BEING A DOG

The world from your dog's point of view

BEING A DOG

The world from your dog's point of view

KAREN WILD

Dip App Psych, CCAB

hamlyn

An Hachette UK Company
www.hachette.co.uk

First published in Great Britain in 2016 by Hamlyn,
a division of
Octopus Publishing Group Ltd
Carmelite House
50 Victoria Embankment
London EC4Y 0DZ
www.octopusbooks.co.uk

ISBN 978 0 600 63150 7

A CIP catalogue record for this book is available from
the British Library.

Printed and bound in China

10 9 8 7 6 5 4 3 2 1

Hamlyn
Editorial Director: Trevor Davies
Editor: Pollyanna Poulter
Designer: Jaz Bahra
Production Controller: Marina Maher

Produced for Hamlyn by
Sarah Tomley @ EditorsOnline.org
Tracy Killick @ Tracy Killick Art Direction & Design

Disclaimer
The advice in this book is provided as general information
only. It is not necessarily specific to any individual case and
it is not a substitute for the guidance and advice provided by
a licensed veterinary or behavioural practitioner consulted
in any particular situation. Octopus Publishing Group Ltd
accepts no liability or responsibility for any consequences
resulting from the use of or reliance upon the information
contained herein.

Unless the information given in this book is specifically for
female dogs, dogs are referred to throughout as 'he'. The
information is equally applicable to both male and female
dogs, unless otherwise specified.

Contents

Introduction

This book looks at the world through the eyes of a dog, to see what it really means to be a dog in today's busy and complicated world. 'Being a dog' is not simply a matter of biology – it's an intricate mesh of genetics, learning, appearance and behaviour, so it is a constantly evolving state of being.

A dog's idea of himself and the external world of people and things around him is continually and profoundly affected by the immediate environment. Living alongside humans, a dog's job may vary from being a gentle companion to guarding livestock, helping people in ill-health or even detecting bombs for the military, where his instincts and tenacity may be tested to capacity.

As an aid to understanding the world from a dog's perspective, this book speaks in a dog's voice to explain why and how dogs make the choices they do. What can a dog see, hear or otherwise sense? Can a dog feel or make decisions? How much of human speech do dogs really understand?

This species has developed evolutionarily in ways that specifically help them live with humans.

The way dogs communicate, tolerate their owners' rules and routines, constantly adapt and learn to enjoy the benefits of this relationship are explored in depth over the course of the book.

A dog's family may include humans, other dogs and perhaps other small animals, such as cats or rabbits. This can affect a dog's development in many ways, both for good or ill, depending on how the situation is handled by the dog's owner. For this reason I have included several sections on decoding dog behaviour, so that owners who may already have strong bonds with their dogs can get to know them even better and make sure they are really meeting their canine companion's needs.

Dogs are exceptionally varied in appearance, as a result of breeding paths that have been deliberately selected by people. These differences fascinate humans. Does the way a dog looks influence the way he behaves, or are there other, equally important factors? Are the working traits that dogs have developed over time now helping or hindering them in modern lives? By examining the evolution of the dog, significant life stages, biological makeup and the significant ways in which they learn from humans, each other and the environment, this book offers a unique window into what it is really like to be a dog today.

Each chapter explores the individual elements involved in being a dog, and the text is accompanied by visual guides that help to deepen understanding still further. Taken together, the elements contained in these chapters add up to a unique and complete picture of what it means to be a member of *Canis lupus familiaris* – or what it is really like, being a dog.

LIVE
BORDERS

1
WELCOME TO YOUR DOGGY WORLD

How do you seem to know when we are upset, happy or excited? How is it we can understand what you mean when you make noises, run, wag your tail and tilt your head in a way that melts a human heart? There is long-standing evidence that your world has intricately evolved alongside ours.

Being a modern dog

Scientists have compared your evolution with that of humans and found significant parallels. Your social standing in human society has extended; you began by providing fur for clothing and acting as a food source, but then you became a working companion and ultimately part of the family.

You have a huge presence worldwide, gathering with people wherever you both settle. Human households around the world have seen a steady increase in dog ownership since the start of the 21st century.

Worldwide populations

Worldwide data is incomplete, because it can be hard to compare surveys of ownership due to differing criteria in data collection. India leads the table for growing dog ownership population (see opposite) even though overall, the country's current dog ownership numbers are still among the lowest in the world. Smaller dogs are increasing in popularity, presumably as lifestyles change to urban settings, but Brazil now has more small dogs per capita than any other country.

Ownership or companionship?

Dogs occupy positions in a broad range of human lifestyles and societies. Breed preferences change as the years pass, but the kind of people who own dogs remains much the same, from single people and families with children to retired couples. However, there has been a demographic shift within these groups. The ageing population of baby boomers (those born immediately following World War II) now own fewer dogs than this age group has done traditionally, suggesting that they find pet care increasingly unfeasible or undesirable. On the other hand, the 'new millennials', or Generation 'Y' (people born between 1982 and 2002) are increasingly choosing to have pets, especially small dogs. In the USA,

the human birth rate fell by 10 per cent between 2007 and 2014, but ownership of small dogs doubled in that time, making them the most popular size of dog. As women in many countries are choosing to give birth later than earlier generations, it seems there is often room for a dog in their homes before children arrive.

Banned dogs

Rules regarding ownership of dogs vary from country to country. Some breeds are banned or restricted (needing muzzles in public); in particular in the UK, Switzerland, Australia and parts of Canada and the USA. Breeds such as the American Pit Bull, Fila Brasileiro, Dogo Argentino, Cane Corso, Rottweiler, various Mastiffs and the Doberman Pinscher are all examples of breeds that are banned in many countries around the world.

Certain breeds may be banned or have restrictions in public such as being kept on the lead or muzzled.

WORLDWIDE DOG POPULATION

There are thought to be more than 500 million dogs in
the world, of which perhaps three-quarters are strays.
Brazil tops the table with around 36 million dogs.

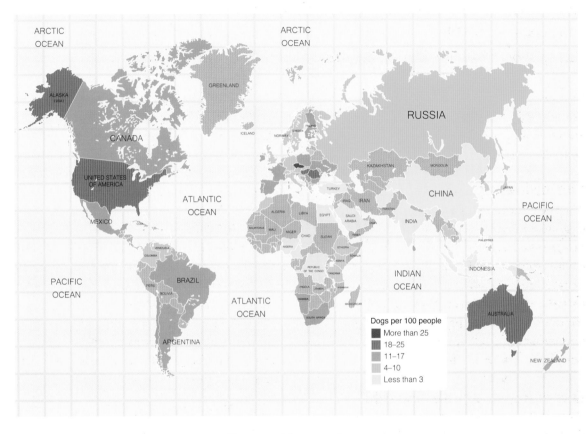

Ownership numbers

In the USA, 36.5 per cent of the population own a dog.
The total pet dog population is estimated at almost
70 million – which means there is one dog for every
four Americans.

In Australia, dogs are owned by 39 per cent of
households and there are an estimated 4.2 million pet
dogs in total. At 19 dogs for every 100 people, they are
the most common Australian pet.

In the UK, dog ownership numbers have remained
relatively stable from 2010-16, with around 24 per
cent of households owning a dog (adding up to around
9 million dogs in total).

Similar numbers exist in Italy and Poland, while
France emerges as a key dog-owning population,
serving as home for more than 7 million dogs. Russia
was recorded as owning the highest number of dogs in
Europe at 12.5 million dogs, while Brazil has the highest
number in the world at nearly 36 million dogs.

Between 2007 and 2012, the number of dogs in India
grew by 58 per cent, making this the fastest growing
population of any country surveyed by Euromonitor
International in 2015 (when it produced reports on 53
countries). Growing urbanization worldwide is likely to
see continued growth in pet companionship.

Your lifestyle

When human families choose you as a companion, they are not only responding to social fashions or looks. You are considered to be a member of the family and are increasingly treated as an important part of this unit. Nearly three-quarters of pet dogs share their owner's bed at night.

As people's lifestyles and incomes improve, their dogs benefit – you'll find they have more time in their lives and space in their houses for you. Their increasingly careful attitude represents good news for your care; there are now more dog walkers, groomers and dog trainers than ever before. You can also expect to be provided with many home comforts that could be considered specifically human, such as recognition of birthdays.

Dogs are different

The phenomenon of anthropomorphism or 'pet humanization' has led to a leap in associated businesses, and commercial products are now available for every need you may (or may not) have. In the USA, 45 per cent of pet owners admit buying birthday gifts for their pets, with 64 per cent buying Christmas gifts. However,

Putting novelty clothes on pets can restrict their ability to express their normal behaviour, or leave them feeling scared or confused.

they may choose gifts with their own tastes in mind, rather than yours. For instance, certain bright colours attract humans, so the products are designed to attract their interest, regardless of a dog's preference (you may actually be more interested in investigating the cardboard box in which the items arrived).

The way that firms now meet your owner's demands for products has changed. Products are no longer only available from your local pet shop. Pet-friendly megastores and more importantly, internet retailing, home improvement stores and even garden centres are places your owner can now buy dog-related goods.

Do dogs need clothes?

This burgeoning consumerism has led to some concern in dog welfare communities. Around 22 per cent of dog owners in the USA state that they dress their pet in some form of clothing, for instance. The phenomenon of 'dog couture' – clothing designed for fashion rather than function – has been criticized by animal welfare organizations who suggest that you cannot express normal behaviour under these restrictions.

A further concern is that you may be viewed as a fashion accessory rather than a living being and a lifelong canine partner. However, hairless breeds of dog such as the Chinese Crested, or lean dogs with a very fine fur, may actually require additional layers to retain warmth even in normal temperature ranges. The question of 'to clothe or not to clothe?' is essentially connected to your breed and environment.

ANTHROPOMORPHIZING DOGS

Many humans make the mistake of thinking that dogs
will share their preferences. This idea is usually mistaken.

Dogs at work

You have been found to have
calming qualities in the workplace.
Owners who take their dogs to work
have been found to show higher
levels of job satisfaction than those
who do not. Stress levels began at
the same level at the start of the
day, but those with dogs showed
decreased levels of stress as the
day went on compared to workers
without dogs.

Sleeping partners

Several studies show that nearly
three-quarters of dog owners allow
their pets to sleep in the bed with
them. This most frequently occurs
in the case of small dogs, less so
for medium sized dogs, and most
rarely for large dogs. Sleeping on
the same bed does not always make
for a peaceful night: some owners
report improved sleep, but others
suffer a disrupted night.

Cooked a special meal

Around 30 per cent of US pet
owners cook for their pets, as they
prefer to make their own choices
about your diet. You might also find
that your owner is keen to offer
celebratory food alongside his own:
according to a 2011 Petplan survey,
62 per cent of dogs in the UK
enjoyed a special Christmas dinner,
and 25 per cent had a specially
cooked birthday meal.

Celebratory presents

For you, a gift might be an
unexpected discovery of fascinating
smells from other dogs, rather than
an item wrapped in paper. However,
66 per cent of pet owners admit
they buy birthday and Christmas
presents as well as accessories for
you to enjoy at these celebratory
times of year.

Someone to talk to

Over half of dog owners chat to you
regularly, describing themselves as
using a 'different' voice to their own
normal speech pattern. Dog owners
are more likely to think their dog
understands them (84 per cent)
than cat owners (73 per cent) or
rabbit owners (61 per cent).

Couture for dogs

Your owner may decide you need
an extra layer of clothing or simply
want you to look 'smart'. In the
2011 Petplan Pet Census, 25 per
cent of pet owners said they had
bought clothing for their pet, with
the highest group being dog owners
(at 36 per cent they far outranked
cat owners at 8 per cent).

How you are built

Your official name is *Canis lupus familiaris*, the domestic dog. You are found worldwide and humans have selectively bred you for many purposes, all of which highlight various aspects of your behaviour and physical attributes. In this chapter we explore your canine construction in detail.

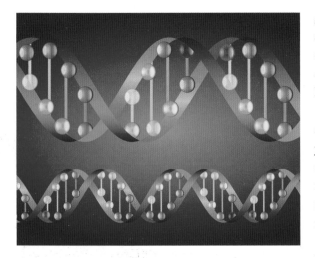

Although dogs and wolves contrast in behaviour and habitat, biologist Robert Waynes compared their mitochondrial DNA sequences and found a 1% difference.

You have 78 chromosomes (39 pairs) compared to 46 (23 pairs) in humans. Your keen senses reflect your complex make-up, and your sense of smell, in particular, far surpasses that of humans. You even have a special sensory organ for scent that allows direct contact with chemical cues such as pheromones, which in turn give you valuable information about other dogs.

Your hearing is very sensitive, and you can hear sounds that are far too faint or high-frequency for humans to detect. This allows you to identify the location of noises, while your emotional reaction to them is shown by the different postures that your ears adopt. Your eyesight has developed to suit your needs, from gazing over long distances to identify moving prey, to be able to focus in on nearby objects (such as your human caregiver's face). On colours, you're less accomplished, seeing only within a limited range that is similar to humans suffering from red-green colour blindness.

Your taste is more limited than humans too: you have around 1,700 taste buds compared to their 10,000. But you enjoy salt, sweet, bitter and sour flavours clustered on the tip of your tongue. Your teeth are far more impressive than humans: you can crush bone to get to the nutritious marrow inside as well as tearing and shredding flesh. You have around 42 teeth as an adult dog.

Vocally, you create a wide range of sounds – barks, howls, growls, yips, huffs – each with a specific meaning. Your barks differ in meaning, such as the one you might give as a 'play invitation' in comparison to your 'stranger approaching' bark. You are likely to have another to communicate to your owner when it is time for a walk.

Bones and organs

Your bones are very strong, and your spine is extremely flexible, bending and stretching easily as you run to catch a toy or prey. Non-retractable claws on your legs act like the spikes on a human sprinter's shoes, giving you great traction. Your legs can be short (allowing easy access to burrows, with large feet for digging), or long (for rapid acceleration when chasing). Some breeds are able to reach 64 km/h (40 mph) or more.

A human heart beats at around 72 beats per minute (bpm). In comparison, a large dog's heart can beat at

60–100 bpm, while a small dog's heart beats at around 100–140 bpm. Your brain structure is similar to that of humans, having the same hormones and undergoing the same chemical changes that human brains do during emotional states. Your brain responds to emotional sounds from other dogs and humans, too.

Different breeds have differing tail lengths, but there is an average of 319 bones in your skeleton compared to 206 in a human. Tails provide a wealth of information about your mood, but a wagging tail does not always mean you are happy. The tension, speed, and positioning of the tail wag is significant and your owner needs to learn what the wag is really saying.

You sleep for an average of 12–14 hours per 24-hour day. Your sleep patterns are similar to that of humans combining both Rapid Eye Movement (REM) and non-REM sleep. Older dogs tend to sleep less at night and have less REM sleep than younger dogs.

ANATOMY OF THE NOSE AND EAR

Designed for smelling

A dog's nasal cavity is divided into two chambers, each containing bony plates called turbinates; these feed sensory information about smells to the olfactory centre in the brain. The nasal cavity also contains Jacobson's Organ, which is able to detect pheromones, providing the dog with information about another dog's availability for mating. The tongue is used for many tasks, including registering tastes, conducting heat, taking up food and water, and healing wounds.

Nose

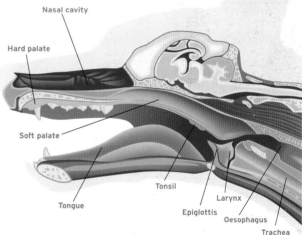

Nasal cavity
Hard palate
Soft palate
Tongue
Tonsil
Epiglottis
Larynx
Oesophagus
Trachea

Ear

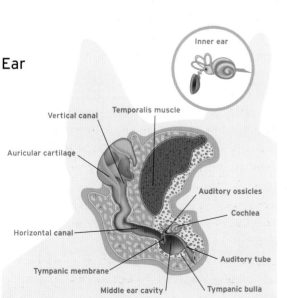

Inner ear

Temporalis muscle
Vertical canal
Auricular cartilage
Auditory ossicles
Cochlea
Horizontal canal
Auditory tube
Tympanic membrane
Middle ear cavity
Tympanic bulla

A finely tuned ear

A dog's ear has three parts: the outer, inner and middle ear. The middle ear is used to process sound, while the inner ear collects information that is vital to the dog's sense of balance. It also helps decode vibrations into meaningful 'messages', which are carried to the brain via the auditory nerve.

Your body

You have evolved to serve multiple purposes. Your body may have developed in particular ways to survive in your local climate and you may have been selected for breeding with other dogs to emphasize specific characteristics. You are, however, uniquely recognizable as 'canine'.

From your skeletal structure to the inner workings of your digestive system, your body works seamlessly when you are in good health. Four of the main systems are shown here (see opposite page), but others, such as the endocrine, lymphatic and urogenital systems are equally important to you. Your respiratory system, including your mouth, nose, lungs and airways as well as your trachea, are essential for absorbing oxygen and for the elimination of waste gases such as carbon dioxide. This system takes on special emphasis as you hardly sweat through your skin; you rely on your respiratory system to regulate body temperature as you pant.

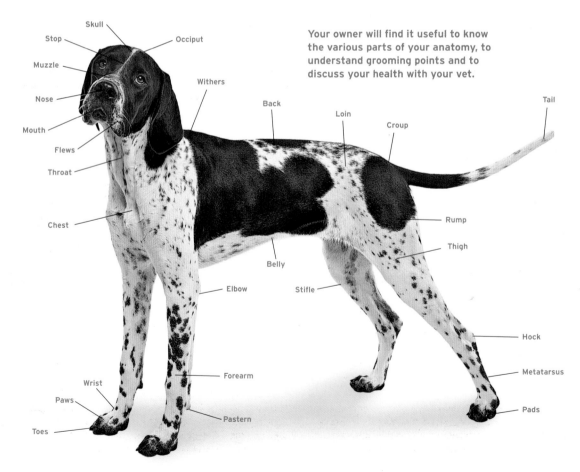

Your owner will find it useful to know the various parts of your anatomy, to understand grooming points and to discuss your health with your vet.

Skull
Stop
Occiput
Muzzle
Withers
Nose
Back
Loin
Croup
Mouth
Tail
Flews
Throat
Chest
Rump
Thigh
Belly
Elbow
Stifle
Hock
Metatarsus
Forearm
Wrist
Paws
Pads
Pastern
Toes

ANATOMY OF THE BODY

Your anatomy is testament to your power as a predator,
and your body has evolved to give you all the skills you
need to track, chase, catch, kill and carry prey.

Skeleton

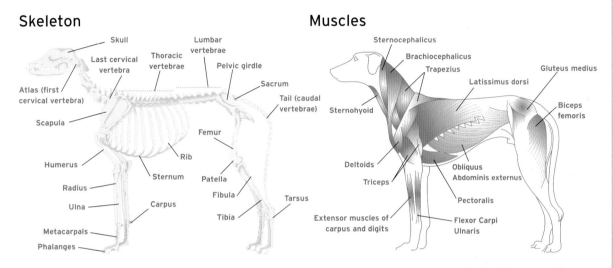

Skull
Last cervical vertebra
Thoracic vertebrae
Lumbar vertebrae
Pelvic girdle
Sacrum
Tail (caudal vertebrae)
Atlas (first cervical vertebra)
Scapula
Femur
Humerus
Rib
Sternum
Patella
Radius
Fibula
Ulna
Carpus
Tarsus
Tibia
Metacarpals
Phalanges

Your spine is extremely flexible, giving you speed and
agility for hunting prey. Your forelegs are attached to
your body only by muscles (you do not have a 'collar
bone') which allows an increased stride length.

Muscles

Sternocephalicus
Brachiocephalicus
Trapezius
Latissimus dorsi
Gluteus medius
Sternohyoid
Biceps femoris
Deltoids
Obliquus Abdominis externus
Triceps
Pectoralis
Extensor muscles of carpus and digits
Flexor Carpi Ulnaris

You have two types of muscle: 'fast twitch', which
allow for great speed; and 'slow twitch', which are more
efficient at burning fat and providing stamina. These
are found in different proportions in dog breeds.

Cardiovascular system

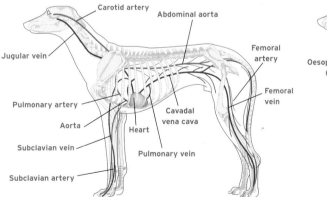

Carotid artery
Abdominal aorta
Jugular vein
Femoral artery
Pulmonary artery
Femoral vein
Aorta
Cavadal vena cava
Heart
Subclavian vein
Pulmonary vein
Subclavian artery

Your heart and blood circulatory system function
very like a human's. However, your paws use a special
mechanism called 'counter current heat exchange' to
keep them warm (this is also found in penguins' feet).

Digestive system

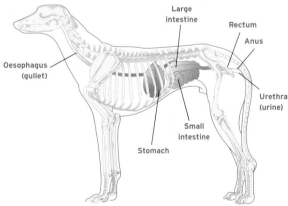

Large intestine
Rectum
Anus
Oesophagus (gullet)
Urethra (urine)
Small intestine
Stomach

You swallow food in large chunks, without chewing, as
your digestive tract is designed for processing meat
(you can digest meat faster than plants). Meat passes
through you (from eating to elimination) in 8-9 hours.

Your brain

Brain-imaging studies have revealed that you study faces in much the same way as humans, and seem to process voices and emotion in a similar way too. This is because you have brain systems that are devoted to making sense of vocal sound, and can distinguish emotional content.

People share many brain functions with mammals, but dogs share some particular cognitive skills with people. Scans indicate that you have a particular area of the brain (the temporal lobe) in which you can process facial information. You are also able to determine an image of an angry face from a happy one, even with faces that are unfamiliar to you, but what you interpret from this is still uncertain. However, studies by scientists at Lincoln University, UK, have indicated that you look more to the right-hand side of a human's face, gaining information that indicates the emotional state of the individual. This is because the left hemisphere of the brain is more involved in emotionally charged information, which is then displayed on the right-hand side of human faces.

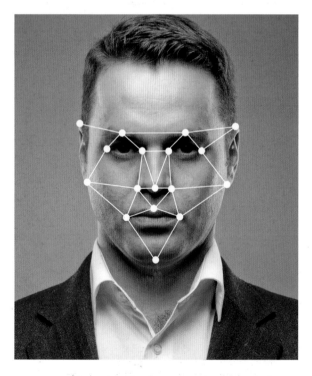

You show more interest in scanning faces that you know than those that are unknown to you, and seem to be able to scan and recognize facial features much as humans do.

You study human faces, possibly for signs of intention or emotion, but studies have shown that you prefer viewing the faces of other dogs more than human ones.

HUMAN BRAIN VS DOG BRAIN

Recent brain-imaging research has found striking similarities between human and dog brains, including the way both mammals process voice and emotion.

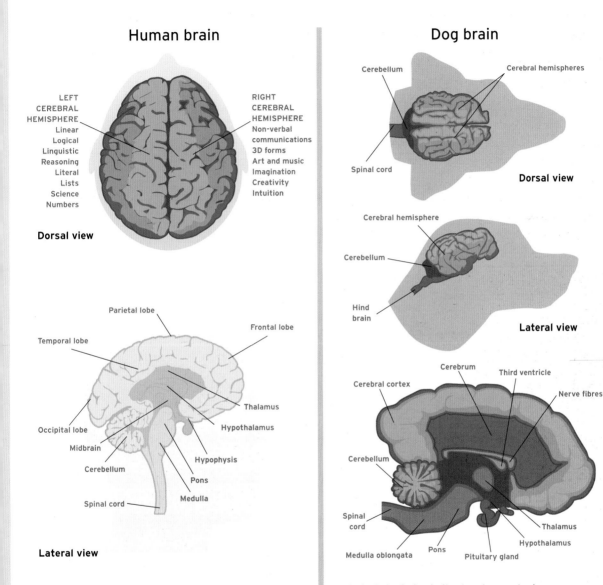

Human brain

Dorsal view

LEFT CEREBRAL HEMISPHERE
Linear
Logical
Linguistic
Reasoning
Literal
Lists
Science
Numbers

RIGHT CEREBRAL HEMISPHERE
Non-verbal communications
3D forms
Art and music
Imagination
Creativity
Intuition

Lateral view

Parietal lobe
Frontal lobe
Temporal lobe
Thalamus
Hypothalamus
Occipital lobe
Midbrain
Hypophysis
Cerebellum
Pons
Medulla
Spinal cord

Dog brain

Dorsal view

Cerebellum
Cerebral hemispheres
Spinal cord

Lateral view

Cerebral hemisphere
Cerebellum
Hind brain

Cerebrum
Third ventricle
Cerebral cortex
Nerve fibres
Cerebellum
Spinal cord
Thalamus
Hypothalamus
Medulla oblongata
Pons
Pituitary gland

Brain activity in humans when in contact with dogs has been found to be very similar to their reaction to children; both dogs and babies spark activity in brain regions associated with visual processing, social interaction, emotion, affiliation and reward.

A dog's brain is similar to a human brain in important ways; functional MRI studies have shown that they both process emotionally laden vocal sounds in a similar way. Happy sounds light up the auditory cortex in both species.

Your ancestors

Evidence indicates that your extended family 'Canidae' (carnivorous mammals including foxes, jackals, wolves and dogs) has spread across 50 million years to the present day. Canids are found on all continents with the exception of Antarctica.

Your ancestry

Within the Canidae family, there are three distinct groupings as well as some, like the raccoon dog, that have a separate lineage (see opposite page). Fox-like canids such as the arctic fox, red fox and fennec fox are members of the *Vulpes* genus, and descend from the ancient *Leptocyon*. Wolf-like canids such as the dog, grey wolf and coyote are members of the *Canis* genus, and evolved from the *Curyon Davisi*, a species that existed during the late Miocene period (7 million years ago). This category also includes the African hunting dog and South-American canids such as the bush dog and maned wolf. You resemble some of these more than others, but they are all your distant cousins.

Scientific evidence

Genetic investigation shows that you descended from wolf-like ancestors, with domestication exerting considerable influence in more recent times, apparently shaping your morphology and behaviour to the companion dog you are today. Until recently, it was thought that dogs evolved around 15,000 years ago, but recent studies of mitochondrial DNA sequences have indicated that dogs may have been present both during and after the lifetime of grey wolves. Such findings would give you an origin of 40,000–135,000 years ago. This data is under scrutiny and critique; at present it is very much debatable but study continues.

How you differ to a wolf

As a dog, you differ physically from wolves in many ways. Physiologically, you have a blunter snout, shorter front-skull, smaller body size and comparatively crowded teeth. Wolves and dogs both develop a sense of smell by around two weeks of age, hearing at four weeks, and vision at around six weeks. However, wolves begin to explore their environment earlier – at two weeks of age – using their sense of smell to guide them. This may represent a critical difference in your social learning, as the socialization 'window' closes earlier for the young wolf cub.

Wolves and dogs share visual similarities and some behavioural similarities but they are vastly different in terms of their domestication and interactions with humans – especially their companionship.

THE CANINAE

It is argued that canines lived only in North America until around 6 million years ago, when geological changes created bridges between Asia and North America, and all the Americas. This allowed canines to spread to new continents.

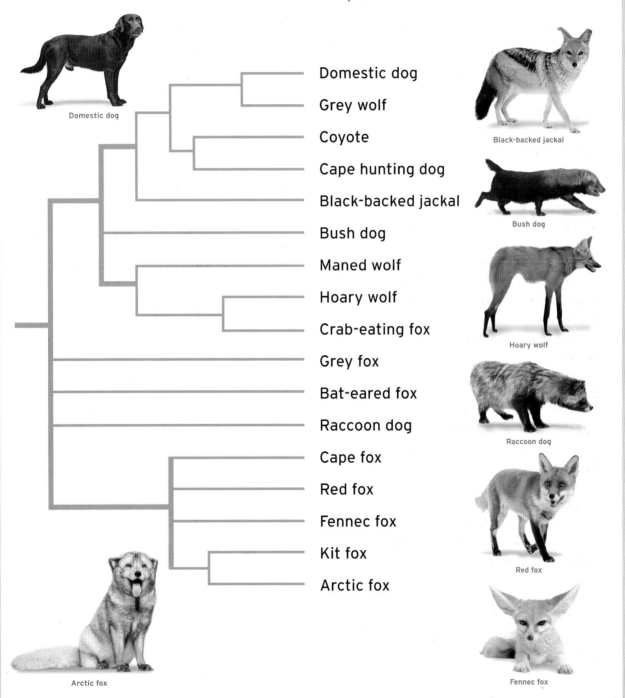

Domestic dog

Black-backed jackal

Bush dog

Hoary wolf

Raccoon dog

Red fox

Arctic fox

Fennec fox

Domestic dog

Grey wolf

Coyote

Cape hunting dog

Black-backed jackal

Bush dog

Maned wolf

Hoary wolf

Crab-eating fox

Grey fox

Bat-eared fox

Raccoon dog

Cape fox

Red fox

Fennec fox

Kit fox

Arctic fox

Your evolving form

Science has demonstrated that you diverged from wolves thousands of years ago, and have a long history of evolution. Your natural evolution has been distorted in recent times by deliberate breeding choices; you may have developed very differently if humans had not become involved.

A long history of evolution led to more than 215 species of canidae over the course of 40 million years, when the Hesperocyon – the ancestor of all canids – first roamed the Earth. One of its subspecies was Borophaginae, a smaller, fox-like predator that lived from 32 to two million years ago. Another subspecies, Caninae, arose at around the same time, and these are the only canids to survive to the present day (see page 21).

Adapting to survive

It is thought that as climate changes occurred to the surroundings, with the dense forest changing to more spacious areas, the canid movement styles changed from lying-in-wait ambush at close range to long distance predatory pursuit. Your ancestors' joints altered to permit paws to face downwards. This new direction replaced paws that used to swivel inwards and was more suitable for pouncing on target prey in the previous, wooded location. Teeth became more durable, hinting that the prey your ancestors needed to deal with were also impacted upon by the change in environment.

All the canids have similar body shapes, and are recognizable for their upright ears (placed high on the head), bushy tails, long legs (allowing tracking and pursuit) and long muzzles (containing teeth that can tear animal hide and break bones apart to get to the marrow within). You have many features still relating to your ancestors, even if humankind has bred you to look rather different in relatively recent times. This explains why you still find it easy to tear your toys apart.

The Borophagus developed extremely enlarged fourth molars to assist in the cracking of bones.

Evolving alongside humans

Just as you evolved to survive and manage in your changing environment, humans did too. Climate changes and limited resources meant that both humans and your dog ancestors had to hunt well to survive. Humans probably recognized the benefits of a companion that had a remarkable scenting ability, great persistence and a hunting instinct. A long-lasting bond was created.

Humans later began to breed dogs to reflect the jobs they wanted them to do, from hounds for hunting, shepherding dogs for guarding flocks, and mastiff-type dogs (such as the Ancient Greek Molossus) for guarding the home. There is evidence that the Egyptians were breeding Saluki-type hounds as far back as 2000 BCE. Breeders then began to look for ways to increase strength, speed, stamina and scenting ability. This gave rise to the rich number of dog breeds today.

A POWERFUL ANCESTRY

Of the 214 species of canids that have ever existed, only 37 survive today. The great ancestor of all of these was the Hesperocyon, which lived for 25 million years in North America. Modern dogs can trace their ancestry to two of its descendants – the Borophaginae and the Caninae – powerful, predatory, carnivores.

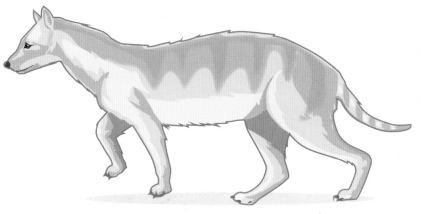

Hesperocyoninae

This small, primitive canid first appeared 40 million years ago, becoming extinct 25 million years later. The main sign of it being a canid is its development of a protective outer ear housing and delicate middle-ear bones.

Borophaginae

These lived from 32 to 2 million years ago. They were small to medium sized, and developed from a larger group of canids (the Borophagus) who developed strong bone-crushing teeth.

Caninae

This is the only subfamily of the Canidae still living. The canines arose 32 million years ago, and dispersed widely, reaching Eurasia, Africa and the entire New World by 13,000 BCE.

A domesticated animal

You are described as a 'domesticated' species. Domestication not only means being trained or bred to work with humans, but also relates to the process of adaptation to a home environment. Your ancestry fits neatly into both descriptions, and you were bred for food and fur.

You are said to be the first domesticated species, and you may have played an important part in the human transition from the hunter-gatherer lifestyle to settled farmer, with captive livestock and managed crops. However, the facts are far from clear. Did you originate from one population of dogs, or multiple stocks? And when did this take place? Research has been unable to situate your domestication accurately, and can only suggest that it occurred 11,000–32,000 years ago. Three

separate areas are believed to be locations from which the domestic dog originated; South-East Asia, the Middle East and Europe, although this is still debated.

Who was your direct ancestor?

A prehistoric wolf-like animal from the Siberian Taimyr Peninsula is considered to be the most likely ancestor of both domestic dogs and modern wolves. It is thought that your predecessors split from their wolf-like ancestors 9,000–16,000 years ago, which would place this before humans switched to agricultural farming.

In 2014, a multi-national team of scientists (A.H. Freedman *et al*.) compared the genome sequences of an Australian Dingo, a Boxer dog and an African Basenji, along with Grey Wolves from China, Croatia and Israel (three regions where dogs were believed to have originated). The three dogs were found to relate to one another more closely than they did to the modern wolf. The research also showed that Greenland sled dogs and Siberian Huskies shared a large number of genes with their Siberian ancestor, so a Husky alive today has a direct DNA link to its 35,000-year-old ancestor. A 2015 examination by Harvard scientists Skoglund *et al.* into the origin of 'village dogs' (those that live in and around human settlements today) showed that they were direct descendants of the dogs domesticated 15,000 years ago.

The wolf and the domestic dog are distinct species and not considered to be alike in behaviour. The wolf-like ancestor from which you both originated is believed to be long extinct.

ANCESTRY AND WORKING ROLES

Dogs and wolves began with a common wolf-like ancestor, but dogs evolved separately into the specific breeds we now recognize. Ancient Asiatics such as the Chow Chow and Akita are thought to evolve separately from European breeds including the Golden Retriever and Corgi. However this research is under debate.

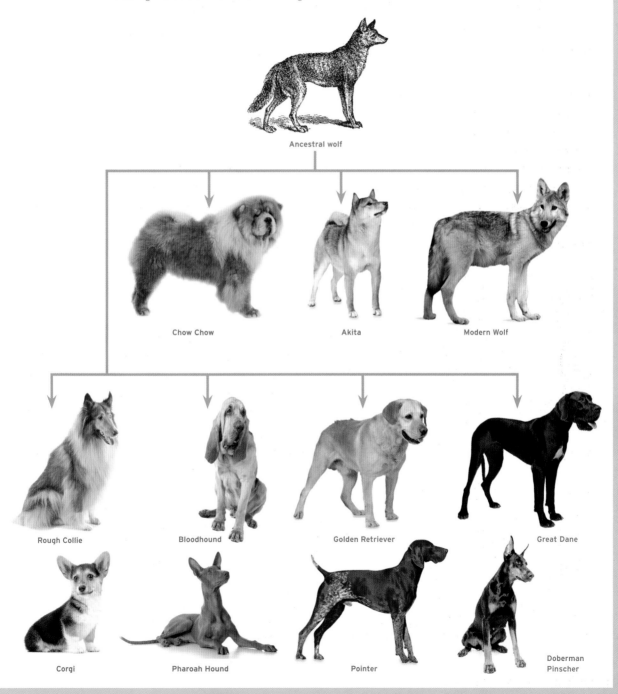

Ancestral wolf

Chow Chow

Akita

Modern Wolf

Rough Collie

Bloodhound

Golden Retriever

Great Dane

Corgi

Pharoah Hound

Pointer

Doberman Pinscher

How you lived with humans in the past

Modern dog owners are not the first humans to have brought you into their families and granted you companionship status. Records indicate that in ancient times, many humans considered dogs to be significant in their lives and referred to them in much the same way as family members.

The importance of your companionship has been frequently recorded. Even in ancient times you were granted access to homes, allowed to share shelter and resources, and treated to specially produced items such as collars. Sheepdogs were given studded leather collars, known as *melium* in Ancient Greece, to protect their necks from the bite of a wolf as they tended their flock.

Dogs in Ancient Rome

In his engaging book *Society and Politics in Ancient Rome*, Frank Abbott mentions some epitaphs from Roman times that describe the pet-owner relationship. Patricus,

a dog, received this tribute from his grieving mistress at Salernum: 'In thy qualities, sagacious thou wert like a human being… Thou, sweet Patricus, wert wont to come to our table, and in my lap to ask for bits in thy flattering way. It was thy way to lick with eager tongue the dish which oft my hands held up to thee, the whilst thy tail didst show thy joy.' It seems that it is not just you and your modern counterparts who try begging at the dinner table!

In the *Corpus Inscriptionum Latinarum*, a collection of inscriptions from the Roman Empire, there are many that refer to dogs. Your forebears caused as much grief to humans upon their death as the departure of a dog does

In this boar-hunting scene from Ancient Rome, dog and man can be seen acting as hunting companions.

The 15,000 prehistoric rock paintings found at Tassili N'Ajjer, Algeria show many representations of life at that time, including men and dogs working together.

even now. One reads: 'I am in tears, while carrying you to your last rest place as much as I rejoiced when bringing you home in my own hands 15 years ago'.

Ancient breed types

Breed names for dogs in these times tended to reflect geographical location, as well as the role played by the dog. Hunting, draughting (pulling carts), guarding and working sheep were common jobs. These tasks were not the only reasons dogs were kept; there were also performing dogs and pet dogs, and it is clear that these categories overlapped. You fulfilled many roles for humans then, just as you do today.

Smaller dogs were favoured companions, with records noting the *Melitaean* or Melitan dog. Greek records refer to it as the Melitaion kunidion, a small, snub-nosed and usually white lap dog, presumed either to have come from Malta or Mljet in Croatia. Depictions show a curled tail,

This manuscript from the Middle Ages shows (from top to bottom): a sheepdog, hunting dogs chasing their prey, and a dog mourning his murdered master.

sharp muzzle and thick coat. It looks much like today's Spitz-type breeds, although there is no clear link.

Evidence suggests that in medieval times, dogs and other animals were defined by their role, whether this was an indoor companion (kept for amusement) or an outdoor worker (for helping humans in their daily tasks). Spaniels were chosen to serve both functions, but Greyhounds were also popular. It is notable that descriptions of pets at this time referred to size, coat length and colour rather than breed names.

Categorization of breeds

Many of today's dog breeds are the result of deliberate choices made by humans, who favour certain characteristics in dogs and wish to see them repeated. This has resulted in certain 'breed standards' which are exact specifications of size, looks, coat and temperament.

Some breeding combinations can lead to genetic problems, especially when related dogs are bred together, so some countries have introduced licensing to prevent inbreeding. The 'pedigree' of each dog reflects parentage, grandparents and other relatives, and it is intended to maintain desired characteristics while eliminating unwanted ones.

The 'ideal' for any dog depends on the life you are to lead and the skills required, hence standard categorizations can reflect these abilities. Herding, Sporting or Non-sporting, Hound, Working and Toy are common categories, although these vary among countries worldwide. Of course, no one told you, the dog, which category you should fit into – and you may have the looks of a herding breed, the agility of an athletic type, and the working instinct of a lap dog.

The PDSA (People's Dispensary for Sick Animals) in the UK suggests crossbreeds as pets because these are usually free from breed-related health problems. Pedigree dogs have well-documented health problems and potential owners need to consider these carefully before buying one of these dogs. Crossbreeds where both parents have a health issue may also need testing to check whether this is a hereditary condition.

The Five Freedoms of Animals

In 1979, the Farm Animal Welfare Council (a UK government agency) drew up a list of five essential conditions for animals living under human control.

Freedom from hunger or thirst	Access to fresh water and a proper diet to maintain full health
Freedom from discomfort	Access to an appropriate environment, shelter and a comfortable area to rest
Freedom from pain, injury or disease	Help in the prevention or early diagnosis and treatment of disease or injury
Freedom to express normal behaviour	Provision of adequate space, appropriate facilities and the company of conspecifics
Freedom from fear and distress	Provision of conditions and treatment that prevent mental suffering

KENNEL CLUB STANDARDS

A 'Breed Standard' is the guideline that describes the ideal characteristics, temperament and appearance for a particular breed and ensures that the breed is fit for function. This page shows some of the UK Breed Standard details for a German Shepherd Dog.

Ears Medium-sized, firm in texture, broad at base, set high, carried erect, almost parallel, never pulled inwards or tipped, tapering to a point, open at front. Never hanging.

Head and Skull Proportionate in size to body. Cheeks forming softly rounded curve. Skull approximately 50 per cent of overall length of head.

Colour Black or black saddle with tan, or gold to light grey markings. All black, all grey, with lighter or brown markings referred to as Sables. Bi-colour: predominantly black, may have tan or gold markings on head, chest, legs and feet; black markings may be present on toes and rear pasterns. Nose black. Undercoat, except in all black dogs, usually grey or fawn.

Eyes Medium-sized, almond-shaped, never protruding. Dark brown preferred, lighter shade permissible. Expression lively, intelligent and self-assured.

Mouth Jaws strongly developed, with a perfect, regular and complete scissor bite (upper teeth closely overlapping lower teeth) and set square to the jaws. Teeth healthy and strong. Full dentition of 42 teeth is desirable.

Neck Fairly long, strong, with well-developed muscles, free from throatiness. Carried at 45-degree angle to horizontal, raised when excited, lowered at fast trot.

Forequarters Shoulder blade and upper arms equal in length, well muscled and firmly attached to the body. Shoulder blades set obliquely (approximately 45 degrees) laid flat to body.

Body Chest fairly deep (45–48 per cent of height at shoulder), ribs well-formed and long. A 'straight-backed' breed type is now preferable to this sloping back.

Feet Rounded toes well-closed and arched. Pads well-cushioned and durable. Nails short, strong and dark in colour.

Tail Bushy-haired, reaches at least to hock; ideal length reaching to middle of metatarsus. At rest, tail hangs in slight sabre-like curve; when moving raised and curve increased, ideally never above level of back. Short, rolled, curled, generally carried badly or stumpy from birth, undesirable.

Size	Ideal height (from withers and just touching elbows) for dogs is 63 cm (25 in) and for bitches is 58 cm (23 in). Variation in height of above or below 2.5 cm (1 in) of the ideal is permissible.
Temperament	Steady of nerve, loyal, self-assured, courageous and tractable. Never nervous, over-aggressive or shy.

Form or function?

Nature and nurture are linked, but people often make assumptions about you according to your breed, suggesting that this influences your actions. As a result, some breeds of dog are labelled as 'dangerous' even from puppyhood. This is a misguided pre-judgement that should be avoided.

You may look very different from your canine counterparts. Humans can be heard to say they 'prefer' one breed of dog to another, perhaps forgetting that you are all descended from the same ancestors and are still the same species: *Canis Familiaris*. Is it possible that along with looks, you have inherited other genetic traits that can influence how you act?

Along with domestication, your ancestors have undergone change through artificial selection, leading to the development of distinct populations. Selective mating of dogs according to human choice means

that dogs have become breeding partners for specific (human) reasons. In the past, your ancestors' form may have been based on function and purpose. Humans at the time may have needed hunting dogs (such as the Borzoi and Russian Wolfhound), guard dogs (like the Mastiff), or dogs for carrying heavy loads (St Bernards were often used for this purpose). Spaniels were bred in Ireland during the Middle Ages for falconry.

Dog breeds

Domestic dogs display greater levels of behavioural and morphological diversity than have been recorded for any land mammal. Over 340 dog breeds have been registered worldwide. Since relatively small numbers of genes appear to control significant aspects of form and shape, it is possible that the same applies to canine behaviours.

Groundbreaking research begun by Russian geneticist Dmitry Belyaev in the late 1950s involved the selective breeding of silver foxes. Those that showed signs of natural approach to their carers and other signals of 'tameness' were allowed to breed, while those that showed signs of fear or aggressive behaviour were not bred on. Surprisingly, the scientists observed that within a few generations the foxes began displaying social behaviours. They tried to lick their carers and even whimpered to attract attention. Most exciting of all, the foxes' fur changed colour, their ears became more floppy, and their skulls changed shape. It appeared that by selecting for certain dog-like behaviour traits, the foxes' appearance also became more 'dog-like'.

Your appearance has been specifically engineered by breeding, giving huge variation within your species.

GENETIC DISTANCES

The incredible diversity of breed type was comprehensively analysed by Vaysse *et al.* in 2011 and is shown below in the form of a neighbour-joining tree. This shows the raw genetic distances representing relationships between breed samples.

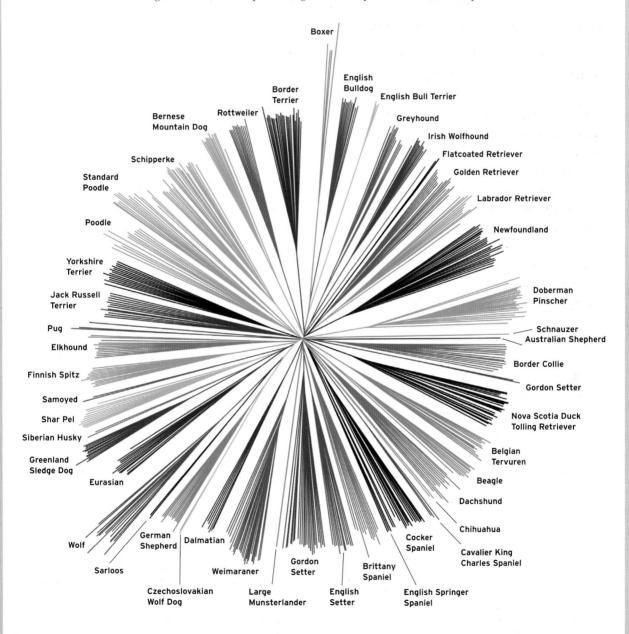

Boxer

English Bulldog

English Bull Terrier

Border Terrier

Greyhound

Rottweiler

Irish Wolfhound

Bernese Mountain Dog

Flatcoated Retriever

Schipperke

Golden Retriever

Standard Poodle

Labrador Retriever

Poodle

Newfoundland

Yorkshire Terrier

Doberman Pinscher

Jack Russell Terrier

Pug

Schnauzer
Australian Shepherd

Elkhound

Border Collie

Finnish Spitz

Gordon Setter

Samoyed

Nova Scotia Duck Tolling Retriever

Shar Pei

Siberian Husky

Belgian Tervuren

Greenland Sledge Dog

Beagle

Eurasian

Dachshund

Wolf

Chihuahua

German Shepherd

Dalmatian

Cocker Spaniel

Cavalier King Charles Spaniel

Sarloos

Gordon Setter

Brittany Spaniel

Weimaraner

Czechoslovakian Wolf Dog

Large Munsterlander

English Setter

English Springer Spaniel

Identification of genomic regions associated with phenotypic variation between dog breeds using selection mapping (Vaysse *et al.*, 2011)

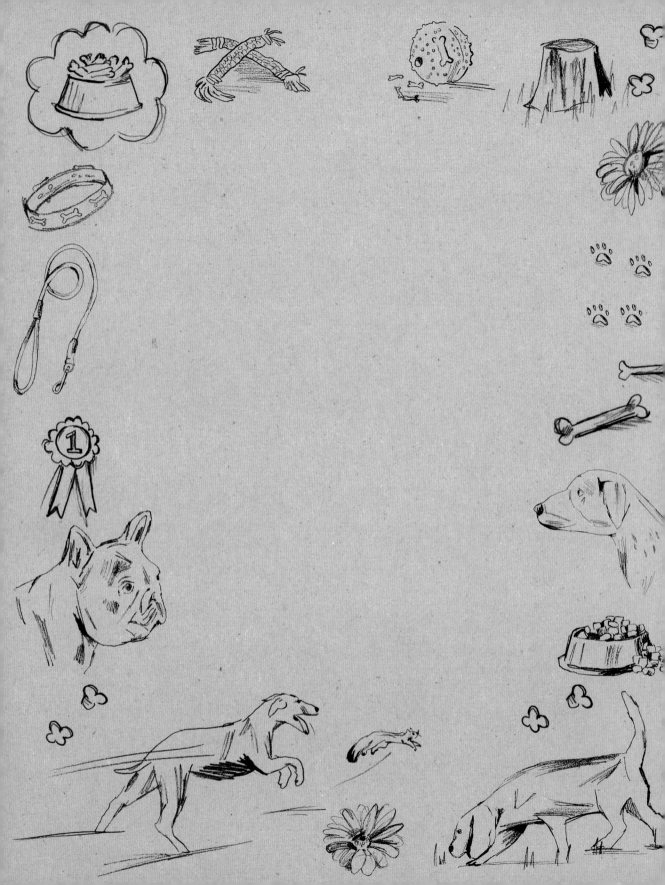

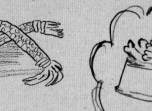

2
HOW YOU SEE AND SMELL THE WORLD

Your incredible sight and scent abilities truly set you apart from humans. In this chapter, we explore your amazing olfactory and visual talents.

What can you see?

Your eye is uniquely adapted to meet your canine needs. Under the low-light conditions of dawn and dusk – your favourite hunting time – you can see far better than humans. You are not able to see as many colours as them, but your other senses more than make up for this lack of information.

Most dogs have brown eyes, but you may have blue ones, or even one brown and one blue if your coat is a merle pattern. You have a third eyelid, known as the 'nictitating membrane' at the bottom of the inner eye. Usually this is hidden beneath the lower lid, but if your eyes are infected or irritated it becomes apparent. Occasionally the gland in the third eyelid can slip out of place and bulge; this condition is known as 'cherry eye' and will need urgent veterinary treatment. It is a hereditary condition, commonly found in Newfoundlands, Bloodhounds, Cocker Spaniels and Beagles, among others.

Dichromatic vision

For many years people assumed that dogs could not see colour, but this is not true. The receptors in a mammal's eye retina are made up of rods and cones: cones detect

The merle gene is responsible for producing a wide variety of coat colours, and often differently coloured eyes.

colour and handle day-time vision, while rods are reponsible for peripheral and night-time vision. Humans and primates have three cones, so they are known as trichromats; as a dog, you have only two, so you are a dichromat. This means that your retina lacks the cones for distinguishing red and green and so it is similar to the retina of a human who is red-green colour blind. However, colour is distinguishable to you, and you have been found to make decisions based on what colour an item is. Dogs who were tested on choosing between yellow and blue, in both light and dark shades, were found to make choices based on the difference in colour, rather than brightness alone.

Colour may not have been important to your survival, compared to your ability to hunt using your other senses. You are able to determine the difference in shades of grey more precisely than humans, which reflects your need to see well in the dusky light of dawn or dusk, when you prefer to hunt. This means that your owner may find it hard to spot you on an early morning or evening walk as you caper off into the distance, while you can easily find your way thanks to your superior vision under these poorly lit conditions.

Navigating by scent

If you lose your sight, it does not have the devastating impact your owner might imagine. You are still able to use your other senses to navigate, because they deliver a multi-dimensional picture to your brain. Dogs that are born blind still survive and make great pets.

HUMAN VISION

DOG VISION

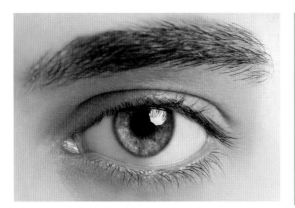

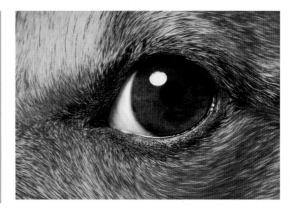

Colour range

Humans have three colour receptors in their eyes, allowing them to distinguish across the full colour spectrum. However, they have fewer cones in their eyes than dogs, so have poorer visual ability in low-light conditions.

The lack of a third colour receptor in the eye means that you're akin to a colour-blind human who is unable to differentiate between red and green. This means that chasing a red ball across a green field is more challenging for you than your owner may expect.

Seeing near and far

Your human owner may wonder why you tip and tilt your head when attempting to see things that are directly in front of you. This is because dogs do not have a fovea in the eye, as humans do, for seeing detail. Instead, you rely on a visual streak that lies at the back of your retinas.

Your eyes work rather like that of humans. They focus on objects near and far, continuously adjust the amount of light that is allowed in and relay all the information gained to the brain for interpretation.

'Visual acuity' is the ability of the eyes to focus – to see the details of an object separately and without blurring. It depends on the ability of the eye to generate a focused image, using the retina to detect and process images, and visual pathways in the brain to interpret what you are seeing. Visual acuity is relatively weak in dogs compared to humans, because they lack a fovea, which allows detailed central vision. Instead, most dogs have a 'visual streak', which is a straight, high-density line of visual cells across the back of the retina that provides extraordinary peripheral vision. This is also used in tracking motion across the peripheral field – an important skill for a predator chasing moving prey (see pages 38–39 for more information).

Visual acuity is tested using a black-and-white striped pattern. Placed next to a uniform grey pattern, a dog can demonstrate his visual ability by picking out the striped pattern for a treat reward. The narrower the stripes, the more difficult the test (rather like making letters smaller on a human test of vision).

Field of vision

While humans can see an image reasonably well at 23 m (75 ft), you will begin to struggle from around 6 m (20 ft) away. On the other hand, your large pupils and wide field of vision – around 240° compared to humans' 180° – means you can even spot some things that are going on behind you. This visual field overlaps at the front, giving you good depth perception. Dogs with a shorter muzzle have better binocular vision, because there is literally less 'nose' in the way. Breeding that is focused on other features may neglect visual ability.

The finer lines on the left show the detail available to a human with 20/20 visual acuity, standing 2 m (6½ ft) away. Those on the right show what an average dog, with 20/75 vision, would see at the same distance.

BREADTH OF VISION

Field of vision

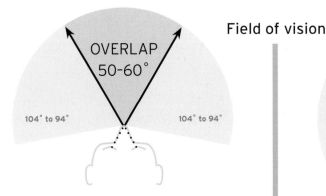

OVERLAP
50-60°

104° to 94°   104° to 94°

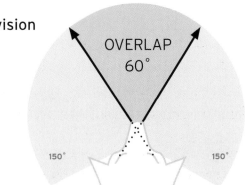

OVERLAP
60°

150°   150°

Humans have eyes on the front of their heads and a fovea that focuses on the detail of objects straight in front of them. Their eyes have around a 180° field of vision and their binocular (3D vision) is broader than that of a dog.

As a dog, your field of vision is greater, thanks to the positioning of your eyes and your visual streak. This allows detection of movement even behind you, which may be key to survival. Your binocular vision is less than a human's but differs between breeds.

Visual focus

A human with good visual acuity (20/20 vision) can clearly see objects close up as well as distant objects on the landscape.

Your 20/75 visual acuity means that while humans can clearly see an object at 27.5 m (90 ft) away, your vision blurs beyond around 6 m (20 ft).

Acuity

Acuity is the ability to focus and therefore see detail, so that two things appear as distinct entities. In humans we measure this with an eye chart. Within the full range of mammals, humans have extremely good focus (it is nowhere near that of birds, but impressive all the same).

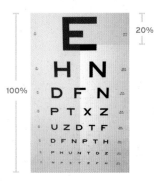

20%

100%

Acuity in dogs is measured using retinoscopy. Depending on the breed, acuity is around 20-40 per cent of that found in humans. However, you don't need to see at close range: your visual abilities for movement and contrast are enough for you to track and chase down what you want.

Tracking motion

On a bright, sunny day, you may surprise your owner by not being able to spot the thrown ball that is now lying right in front of you, but can masterfully locate and chase a squirrel racing across the park. What draws you to this running creature rather than the ball you love to play with at home?

Long-nosed breeds such as the Labrador have very clear peripheral vision, allowing these dogs to locate and follow a moving stimulus across a wide area without moving.

Dogs with short muzzles, such as a Pug, can see objects in front of them quite clearly, but their peripheral vision is less acute than in longer-nosed breeds.

As a dog, you are a cursorial predator, meaning that you evolved to chase down your prey ('cursorial' means 'having limbs that have adapted for running'). The slightest movement in the environment triggers you to give chase, as your system of vision is finely attuned towards detecting motion. You can recognize an object that is moving almost twice as well as you can when the same object is standing still.

As a result, some prey animals have evolved a defence that stops them from moving. The 'freeze' response in rabbits is a means to avoid being noticed by predators who are triggered into attack behaviours by motion. If the rabbit freezes, the motion stops, and the triggering stimulus is interrupted. This explains why you ignore the 'dead' toy once it has landed. Your human, on the other hand, who can easily see the toy, may have to go and fetch it themselves.

Tracking fast movement

The 'optokinetic reflex' refers to the way that eyes reflexively (and involuntarily) track movement. Humans may become aware of this reflex when looking out of a train – the eyes will track the outer landscape for some distance then jump far to the right to begin tracking left again. This reflex is much more sensitive in dogs than humans, and a study by ethologist Ádám Miklósi (2008) found that dogs are able to discriminate moving objects at a distance of 800–900 m (875–985 yd) that they cannot see at 500 m (547 yd) when the objects are stationary. This explains why you might suddenly snap at a fly, or

The flicker-fusion rate is the rate at which the retina updates images to the brain. This is much faster in dogs than in humans, so where humans see seamless motion, dogs see a series of intermittent televized images.

orient your head and body rapidly towards any peripheral movement on walks – even a simple inanimate thing, like a plastic bag blowing in the breeze. It also explains why you may sometimes get into difficult situations, chasing joggers or cyclists who may just keep running, unaware that you are attracted by their rapid movement.

Dogs lack a fovea, which is found in people and other primates inside the macula of the eye, and provides highly focused vision. Instead, most dogs, but especially those with long muzzles, have an oval-shaped, dense 'visual streak' of retinal ganglion cells, which allow the highest visual acuteness for detecting motion. A short-muzzled dog may have virtually no visual streak; instead, the ganglion cells are concentrated in the 'area centralis'. This is a broad central region that has fewer receptors than the human fovea but more than in the peripheral

areas of the eye, so it is good for seeing things close up. So a Retriever, with a long visual streak, has high-quality, panoramic vision, while a Pug, with a greater area centralis, can see things close by much more easily than its long-nosed neighbour.

The attraction of digital TV

You may find you are attracted to movement on television, especially now that it has become digital. This is because dogs have a higher 'flicker-fusion' rate compared to humans. This is the rate at which an animal can take 'snapshots' of the world around them. At around 70–80 cycles per second, your flicker-fusion rate is far superior to the humans' rate of 60 per second. This high rate gives a smoothness to any visual movement – the higher the rate, the smoother the movement is seen to occur.

How you smell the world

Your sense of smell is legendary and it owes much to your physiology. Your nose separates incoming air into separate tracks for determining smell and providing oxygen, and small slits in the nose allow the air scent to exit slowly, so you are able to track scents for up to 210 km (130 miles).

Hound breeds such as the Beagle follow both air and ground scent. The ideal working conditions for tracking scent are cool, moist days without wind or heavy rain.

Your nose may be darkly pigmented, pink or even spotted, and this can change in some dogs depending on the season, becoming darker in summer and lighter in winter ('snow nose'). The surface is usually moist and cool, but can be dry and warm, which may be due to your levels of hydration and activity and the ambient temperature, or it may indicate a fever.

Breathing

Your nose is made from a bony nasal cavity, split into separate chambers by the cartilaginous nasal septum. Inside each cavity sit the 'turbinates' – a labyrinth of thin bones, lined with epithelium tissue and the paranasal sinuses. As you breathe in, your nostrils (nares) flare, changing the shape of the nostril openings. This allows redirection, or splitting, of the air, taking some to the nasal cavities to detect scent and some to the lungs to supply oxygen. As you breathe out, the air is expelled through the slits at the side of each nostril. This causes the air to exit slowly, rendering information and without getting in the way of important incoming odours.

The 'alar fold' sits just inside your nostrils, opening and closing to allowing the air to flow in and out. Should anything tiny, such as dust, obstruct your nose, you will sneeze, but anything larger will need removal by a vet; the delicate and complex interior of your nose can make retrieval difficult.

You usually breathe through your nose rather than your mouth unless you are panting, where this action serves to help you cool down. Brachycephalic breeds (dogs with short muzzles and broad skulls such as Pugs and Bulldogs) may suffer from obstructed breathing, caused by collapsed nostrils and other congenital deformities. As a result, these dogs breathe more through their mouths and tend to snort and snore.

Analysing scent

Your nasal cavity is richly supplied with nerves, linked to the olfactory centre in your brain, where you can keep track of many scents simultaneously. You have around 125–300 million olfactory receptors, compared to a human's six million. Unlike humans, whose noses habituate to smells rapidly, you can analyse and follow a scent for prolonged periods. Humans make use of your enhanced ability by training you to locate things for them,

THE ANATOMY OF SMELL

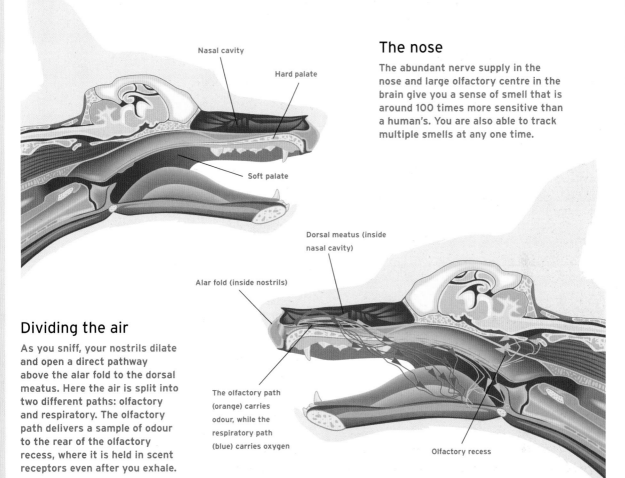

Nasal cavity

Hard palate

Soft palate

The nose

The abundant nerve supply in the nose and large olfactory centre in the brain give you a sense of smell that is around 100 times more sensitive than a human's. You are also able to track multiple smells at any one time.

Dorsal meatus (inside nasal cavity)

Alar fold (inside nostrils)

Dividing the air

As you sniff, your nostrils dilate and open a direct pathway above the alar fold to the dorsal meatus. Here the air is split into two different paths: olfactory and respiratory. The olfactory path delivers a sample of odour to the rear of the olfactory recess, where it is held in scent receptors even after you exhale.

The olfactory path (orange) carries odour, while the respiratory path (blue) carries oxygen

Olfactory recess

from people to contraband (such as drugs and firearms) and disease (such as cancer or diabetes). You sometimes chatter your teeth after licking an area of strong scent such as urine; this is known as 'tonguing', where your tongue is pressed rapidly against the roof of your mouth as the scent is analysed. Some dogs have been seen to 'lick the air' in search of scent.

The vomeronasal organ (also known as Jacobson's organ) in your nose carries information to the brain about emotions and mating. This organ is primarily used to detect pheromones, which are a chemical means of communication between members of the same species and trigger a wide range of responses. Pheromones can communicate sexual factors such as a dog's maturity or the whereabouts of a nearby female on heat, mark territory, or convey aggression. Artificially created dog pheromones are sometimes used by humans to relax and calm dogs who are experiencing stress.

Scent as information

Scent is a significant source of information for dogs. It can be used as a form of communication between animals via long-lasting environmental cues such as urine deposits, faeces and secretions from anal glands. Your human owner has a distinctive scent profile too.

You are able to track scents up to a week old, especially if they have been laid in a cool, damp forest rather than a concreted area with traffic pollution. You are able to interpret scent information from an environment so finely that you discover all sorts of things about people and other animals, from where they have been and for how long, to who they were with and what they have been eating recently. No wonder you are so interested in giving your owner a good sniff when they return home.

Producing smells

Pheromones are chemicals produced by animals that can affect the behaviour of other animals. For instance,

Wild canines rolled in antelope faeces and carrion to disguise their own smell, covering it in a non-threatening one that allowed them to approach prey undetected. This may be a left-over behaviour in domestic dogs today.

female dogs produce a chemical from sebaceous glands in their mammary area shortly after giving birth that is said to have a calming effect on their puppies. This pheromone has been usefully synthesized in products aiming to promote the same impact in an artificial form, in an attempt to help dogs suffering from stress and separation-induced anxiety.

Odour as information

To a dog, every smell is interesting. When you defecate, your anal sacs are stimulated and while it may seem indelicate to your owner, these glands are important to you for individual and territorial reasons. You investigate other dogs' anal regions upon greeting, even when the dogs are familiar friends, and will circle one another in a ritualized sniffing pattern. The anal glands can tell you all about the other dog: what sex it is, how healthy it is, what kinds of things it eats and even what mood it is in.

You may roll in the excrement of other animals or rotting items such as fish. It appears confusing since your sense of smell is so acute; why might you employ this apparently extreme tactic? There are three main theories. It may be that you wish to cover yourself in the stronger scent, supposedly to advertise it to others. Alternatively, you may be attempting to disguise your scent to others. Lastly – and perhaps the most compelling theory of all – you may be demonstrating your ownership of the delicious (to you) aroma, by rubbing your scent onto the target. This might mean that you have scent-claimed it for yourself.

TRACKING SCENTS

Within this 'scent landscape' you will be able to tell whether another dog, human or other creature has passed by; how long ago that was; and in which direction. Is this a dog from your own family, or a stranger?

Humans tend to walk 'heel to toe' providing a heavy impression underfoot that then 'rolls' towards the toe. This allows you to follow the direction in which the human travelled.

The track itself forms from the disturbance of the ground underfoot. Each footprint releases a variety of scents such as crushed grass, compressed soil and so on. Any creature passing by also leaves its own 'tunnel' of scent, which can drift in air currents.

Every movement brings further scent information, not just on leaves (as shown) but also on concrete and tarmac – you are able to track down your target even on these hard surfaces.

A memory for scent

Scent experiments with dogs have proved that your memory allows you to recall scent and this has been demonstrated in search-and-rescue operations as well as obedience competition and tracking. Some breeds appear to have superior scenting ability, but all dogs can track and search.

When you are about to track something down, you are generally given an item that contains the scent of the subject, whether this is a person, animal or object. This may be as little as the human scent left behind on expended cartridge cases, from which police dogs have identified drive-by shooters in the USA.

Finding people

You can both identify scent and then hold it in mind as you search. Dogs are used by the police in many areas

for their scenting ability and other emergency services regularly call on their skills to locate survivors and bodies after disasters such as earthquakes and avalanches. Dogs are also tasked with wildlife conservation purposes, such as seeking turtle nests so that they may be protected. The dogs that are used for these kinds of specific purposes receive intricate, specialized training for their tasks.

The scent you detect varies; when seeking people it may be that you recognize skin cells and respiratory gases. Disturbed ground may indicate the direction of passage: as scent becomes dissipated by the breeze, the classic air scent pattern may see you moving your nose from side to side as you follow the direction in an unmistakable motion. You may lift your head to air-scent or lower it to track along the ground.

Scent breeds

Accuracy is not so much related to breeding as to training and understanding the task required. However, some breeds definitely start with an advantage. The Bloodhound, a breed with 300 million scent receptors, is closely followed by the Basset Hound and Beagle regarding capacity to investigate smell. Their large, elongated heads, long ears, open nostrils and dewlaps (folds of skin around the head and neck) all help in trapping scent. However, individual aptitude and training ultimately count for more than breed type in this area.

A 'trailing dog' is trained to identify and track a specific human odour, as presented to it by its handler.

THE TOP 10 SCENT-TRACKING BREEDS

Bloodhound
1
The Bloodhound's prodigious scent-tracking skills date back to its use in big-game hunting. It has 300 million scent receptors.

Basset Hound
2
The Basset's body sits near the ground, and his long ears sweep any scent upwards towards his keen and powerful nose.

Beagle
3
Beagles have a bigger nose than other dogs their size, 225 million scent receptors and an upright tail that identifies its position even in long grass.

German Shepherd
4
The German Shepherd equals the Beagle in scent receptors, but this dog is best known for his ability to air-scent, catching aromas in the wind.

Labrador Retriever
5
The Labrador has wide uses in communities today. As a trained FBI sniffer dog, it can identify 19,000 different formulations of explosive chemicals.

Belgian Malinois
6
This intelligent dog is highly trainable and is widely employed by emergency services. It has also been used for the detection of prostate cancer.

English Springer Spaniel
7
English Springers have been trained to detect many odours from explosives and narcotics to human remains.

Coonhound
8
The different varieties of Coonhound breeds divide into 'hot-nosed' ones that work best on a fresh trail, and 'cold-nosed' ones that like a cold trail.

German Shorthaired Pointer
9
This gundog shares an ancestor with the Bloodhound and the Spanish Pointer, making it a talented tracking and retrieving dog.

Pointer
10
Pointers were selectively bred to hunt gamebirds such as quail and pheasant. They point with one leg in the direction they smell prey.

3
TASTE, TOUCH AND SOUND

Your senses are keen, but some contribute more to your safety and survival than others. Your owner may be amazed at what you can hear, disgusted at what you eat and delighted that you nudge their hands to get them to stroke you.

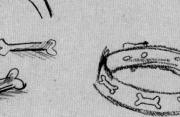

Delicious or disgusting?

Your sense of taste is much weaker than your owner's, because you have only 1,706 taste buds compared to a human's 9,000. On the other hand, you have an extremely efficient sense of smell, so perhaps you don't need to gather so much information once the item is in your mouth.

The number of taste buds that animals have varies enormously: chickens have about 30, while pigs have 14,000 and catfish have up to 175,000, distributed all over their body. You have a general distribution of taste buds across the tongue and, unusually among mammals, you can taste sweetness as well as bitterness. This may be because your sweet taste encourages you to track down furaneol, a natural compound found in plant seeds, which you often and helpfully disperse. By tasting bitterness, you may be warned to avoid decaying or poisonous food. Your tongue has special areas for taste: the front of the tongue has a higher concentration of detectors for salty, sweet and sour tastes, while bitter tastes are detected towards the rear of the tongue.

Taste and poisons

Your owner may react in disgust to your eating habits, as you tend to scavenge and eat an enormous variety of both food and non-food items. Your tongue is used to test palatability and to stimulate your digestive system. And although you can learn that some tastes are aversive and to be avoided, you can (and do) still occasionally eat items that may be harmful to you.

The Veterinary Poisons Information Service (VIPS), based in London, UK, found that in 2014, 10 per cent of the 10,896 pet poisoning cases they dealt with involved eating toxic food. Over 40 per cent of these cases were due to chocolate, which is harmless to humans but lethal for dogs. Cocoa is derived from the roasted seeds of Theobroma cacao, which contains properties that can

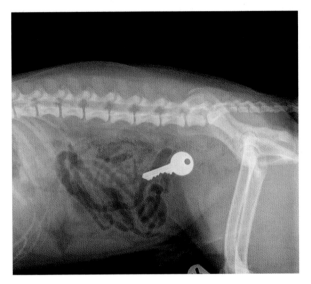

This x-ray clearly shows a key that has become lodged internally (in the colon) after being consumed.

be toxic: caffeine and theobromine. When chocolate is fed at a proportion of 20 mg chocolate per kg (2 lb) of dog weight, it may produce vomiting and diarrheoa in dogs, while seizures can occur at dosages greater than 60 mg/kg. A dose of 28 g/0.5 kg (1 oz/1 lb) of milk chocolate is thought to be a potentially lethal dose for dogs.

Other poisonous foods found to cause problems in large numbers of dogs included grapes, raisins, sultanas, onions and the sweetener xylitol (increasingly used in foodstuffs such as peanut butter). Other harmfully ingested substances included paracetamol, ibuprofen and washing-machine detergents.

COMMON POISONS

These common household items are poisonous to all dogs and must be kept safely out of reach.

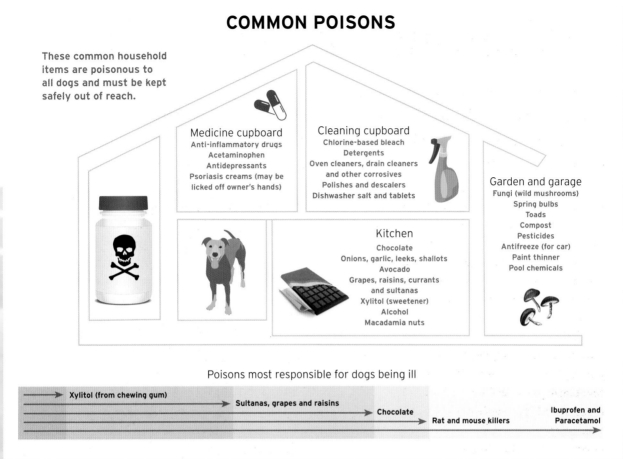

Medicine cupboard
Anti-inflammatory drugs
Acetaminophen
Antidepressants
Psoriasis creams (may be licked off owner's hands)

Cleaning cupboard
Chlorine-based bleach
Detergents
Oven cleaners, drain cleaners and other corrosives
Polishes and descalers
Dishwasher salt and tablets

Garden and garage
Fungi (wild mushrooms)
Spring bulbs
Toads
Compost
Pesticides
Antifreeze (for car)
Paint thinner
Pool chemicals

Kitchen
Chocolate
Onions, garlic, leeks, shallots
Avocado
Grapes, raisins, currants and sultanas
Xylitol (sweetener)
Alcohol
Macadamia nuts

Poisons most responsible for dogs being ill

Xylitol (from chewing gum)
Sultanas, grapes and raisins
Chocolate
Rat and mouse killers
Ibuprofen and Paracetamol

Coprophagia

As a dog, you may enjoy eating non-food items such as stones and plastic. You may also eat animal excrement, which is known as 'coprophagia', which may transfer parasites such as worms to your system, and could be a sign of incomplete digestion. A veterinary check can confirm that you have not been adversely affected, but this habit is rarely a problem for you. Eating a non-food item can result in internal damage, though, and may require emergency and delicate surgery. Even sticks and some bones, so long given out as popular toys for dogs, can perforate internal organs, so are best avoided.

Sounds interesting!

You do not only receive information about your surroundings through your ears; you also use it yourself as a means to communicate. Sound, transferred through vibrations in the air, is collected in the ear flap or 'pinna', which may rotate to help channel sound from its source towards the inner ear.

Breeds that carry the extreme piebald gene, such as Boxers, Dalmatians and English Setters, tend to suffer from congenital deafness due to cochlea degeneration.

Depending on your breed, your ears may be erect or entirely flopped over the sides of your head, and the tips may point upwards or softly bend over. Each ear has hair both on the outside (resembling the rest of your fur) and also on the inside, where it is more sparsely arranged. In some breeds, such as Poodles, the hair can remain thick well down into the ear canal. The shape and angle of the ear canal itself varies, and occasionally moisture can become trapped in this area, leading to infection.

Hearing ranges

Your hearing helps you to register the intention of another dog, identify threatening noises and locate prey, simply by orienting your head and ears. It is difficult to establish exactly what dogs hear, but tests of hearing ranges have helped to indicate which sounds they are able to detect. In experiments, dogs were tested to see if they reacted to a noise stimulus; if they chose the side the stimulus was presented, a dispenser automatically delivered food. An audiogram was then plotted to indicate the point at which the dog began to show signs of hearing, enabling scientists to work out the softest tones that could be heard. It was found that hearing ranges of dogs vary, but they can hear intervals of 67–45,000 Hz, compared to humans, who have a hearing range of 64–23,000 Hz (by comparison a bat can hear from 1,000 to 110,000 Hz, and porpoises up to 150,000 Hz).

Hearing deficiencies

Deafness can occur at any stage of your life. However, there is a genetic component. Hereditary deafness in dogs, particularly congenital (from birth) is often related to white pigmentation and piebald coats; this is most frequently seen in Dalmatians. It can also be unrelated to pigment, as seen in the Doberman Pinscher. It is also possible for late-onset hereditary deafness to occur in Border Collies and Rhodesian Ridgebacks. Hearing loss can occur in a single ear or be bilateral, and it can be total, partial or even peripheral, depending on which part of the inner ear is affected.

THE HEARING RANGE OF ANIMALS

	10 Hz	1 kHz	100 kHz
Tuna			
Chicken			
Goldfish			
Bullfrog			
Catfish			
Cockatiel			
Elephant			
Owl			
Human			
Horse			
Cow			
Raccoon			
Sheep			
Dog			
Ferret			
Guinea pig			
Rabbit			
Sea lion			
Hooded rat			
Cat			
Mouse			
Little brown bat			
Beluga whale			
Bottlenose dolphin			

Naturally sound-seeking

Your world is filled with noises; some are man-made, such as the whirring of your owner's refrigerator or a jet flying overhead. Others, such as the faint scratching of a mouse or the rustling of a hedgehog in the garden, are more natural and can prove irresistible to you as you rush to investigate.

You turn and tilt your head towards an interesting noise to identify its location and likely source.

You use your hearing to help you navigate towards your goal. With your keen sense of hearing, the processing of sounds in your auditory cortex shows that you can tell the difference between sound sources that move and those that are stationary. You can also determine the direction of movement through sound from as early as 16 days old.

You may turn your ears towards the noise, rather like radar dishes, but in your case serving to funnel the sound into your ear. Your owner can use such ear movements to observe where you think the origin of the sound may be. Your head also tilts from one side to another; scientists theorize that this may enable you to see the target better by hearing 'around' your own muzzle, rather than moving your head towards the sound.

Hearing at high pitch

When it comes to high-pitched noises, your hearing vastly exceeds that of your owner. This ability means you make an excellent watchdog, able to warn your owner of impending intrusion well before they would notice. Dogs that have been purposely bred to catch vermin, such as Terriers, are particularly adept at alerting to sounds.

The noises made by rats and mice need acute hearing for humans to detect, whereas a dog can hear the navigational sounds of these vermin even in gardens and behind house walls. Some household items such as digital alarm clocks can emit constant high-frequency sounds, causing distress. Unfortunately your warning bark (across a range of pitches) is often misinterpreted and can become a cause for human complaint.

SOUNDS THAT MAY SCARE

You may tolerate a range of sounds, if you have grown up to become familiar with them.
Some dogs can be upset by sounds such as those shown below.

Cathode Ray Tube and
LCD Displays such as TVs
and computer monitors

Drills, jackhammers,
emergency vehicle sirens

Metallic sounds such as
saucepans clanking, tin
foil rattling, house or car
keys jangling, cutlery

Smoke alarms, burglar alarms

Large home appliances such as lawn
mowers, washing machines, tumble dryers,
paper shredders, heating boilers

Small home appliances such as
whistling kettles, mobile phones,
doorbells, kitchen timers

Sudden, unexplained noises
such as fireworks, thunder,
crackling logs on a fire

Talking dog

You can't resist a bark. What dog can? It's hardwired into you. You bark when you're alone, or excited, scared, angry or even happy. The fact that you bark when you're alone shows that your vocal talents are linked with your emotions as much as they are a necessary means of communication.

Your bark is one thing that clearly separates you from wolves, who rarely bark, as they use stealth to hunt and need to communicate in more subtle ways. Your vocal chords are very flexible, so the timing, pitch and amplitude of your bark can vary considerably.

A growl for any occasion

When presented with different situations you'll respond vocally in different ways. Growls, for instance, are a rather effective form of communication. Researchers have identified a 'food growl', where a dog growls in protection of his meal, and a 'stranger growl' that is emitted on the approach of an unknown human.

When presented with food and played a recording of the two different growls, dogs showed that they weren't worried about the 'stranger growl', but were extremely wary of the 'food growl'. A similar demonstration of aural cognition was demonstrated when a group of dogs listened to a 'stranger bark'. All of them leapt to attention, showing that they understood the meaning of each other's vocal communications. However, the only bark that dog owners could categorically state was different from the rest was the 'stranger' bark.

Silence is golden

With all this yapping, growling, barking and woofing you might think that you're inured to loud noise and even like it, but in fact you prefer the quiet life. In one experiment, two containers of food with bells attached were set before dogs. One set of bells had no clangers. The dogs were commanded to leave this box alone, but were free to feast from the noisier, ringing box. When the researcher's back was turned, every dog pilfered from the 'silent' box.

The scenario	Your common vocal reactions
Protecting a juicy bone	Prolonged growl (1–4 kHz), potentially fierce and followed by a succinct bark.
Approached by a stranger	Forceful, repetitive sharp bark, each lasting 0.2–0.5 seconds, using your full range (1–15 kHz). If feeling threatened, followed by a growl (as above).
Left alone	In younger dogs, short yelps and prolonged high-pitched mewing (more than 12 kHz).
Happy!	Sharp mid-range yaps (jumps and tail wags) which ask to be enjoyed.

THE ANATOMY OF VOCALIZATION

When you vocalize your emotions, you display a wide range of sounds. The pitch varies due to the relative size of the dog, yet the 'shape' of the bark remains the same for each intent, as seen in a sound spectrogram. A bark from a scared puppy will have exactly the same soundscape (or 'shape') as that of a scared adult dog.

Growling

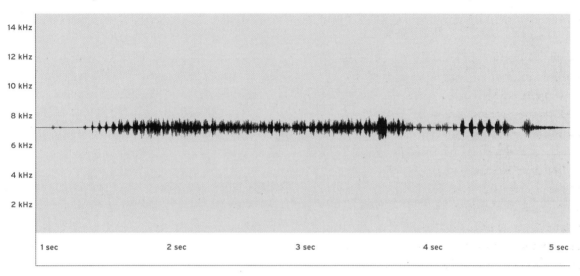

This dog was eating a tasty treat when another dog attempted to steal it. A 'growl' is used by many species to indicate danger and stop another animal from approaching. A growl has a consistent, rumbling tone.

Bark alert

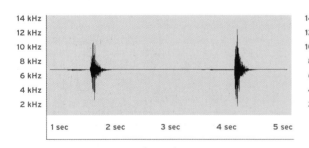

This dog had heard a knock at the door. The 'punch' of sound that occurs with this bark is staccato in nature, tailing off rapidly in readiness for another. An alerting bark is loud, carries over long distances and encourages other dogs to join in.

Howl

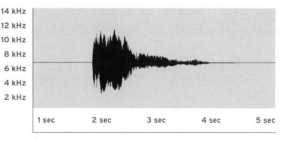

This is the howl of a dog left alone. Howling has a smoother tone than the harshness of barking or growling. The quavering note is held for drawn-out periods.

Responding to sound

You exhibit a degree of innate responsiveness to any sounds your owner makes. This seems to be based on the characteristics of the noise, rather than any words used. Is there a contextual meaning, or particular rhythm that communicates meaning to you?

Sounds with social significance, particularly those made by a human attempting to train you, can elicit changes in your activity levels. For instance, even when you're feeling calm and peaceful, you may become quite excited when asked if you want to go for a walk. An analysis of sound signals used by 100 trainers around the world showed that they shared a universal pattern; similarities were found in the voice tones and type of cues used for specific actions, such as 'Fetch!'.

Trainer tones

In practice, rapid repetition of certain sounds were used by the trainers to speed up the dog. Additionally, clapping of hands, finger snaps, clicking tongue, leg slaps and 'lip smooches' were all used to increase the dog's activity. For calming the mood, long, drawn-out signals such as 'Whoa' were used to slow down or inhibit the dog's activity. It seems that you understand and respond to these particular types of tone and rhythm.

A high-pitched tone was observed to be used by many instructors as a means to gain the dog's attention. This kind of 'signal' – such as two blasts on a whistle – was effective at gaining the dog's attention and directing it on a task. Trainers were found to repeat such noises with increasing speed to help speed up the dog. In another study, one short sound was found to be most effective at eliciting a 'sit–stay' response, and four notes were most effective in getting the puppy to approach. Ascending noises that were rapidly repeated were likened to distress sounds such as yelping and fear.

Owners often disregard the tones of their responses to you. For instance, your owner may wonder why you bark in such a high-pitched tone, but forget that when you do make these sounds, their own efforts to quieten you often mimic your exact high-pitched tone. Effectively they may be encouraging you by joining in!

When you hear a sound, is it the learned cue that you respond to, or the pitch of the sound?

TRAINED TO RESPOND TO SOUND

Sound specific

You innately respond to certain sounds, but you need to be trained to link them with a response. You may learn to link the word 'come' with running back to your owner, but this command also has to stop you doing something, like chasing or sniffing. So the noise must both attract you and interrupt your current behaviour. This can be taught by giving you rewards for returning.

It's not what you say, but how you say it

The three sonograms (sound graphs) shown below show frequency or pitch on the vertical axis and time on the horizontal one. They illustrate the types of sounds that correlate with the expected response from working domestic dogs, as demonstrated by animal behaviourist Patricia McConnell.

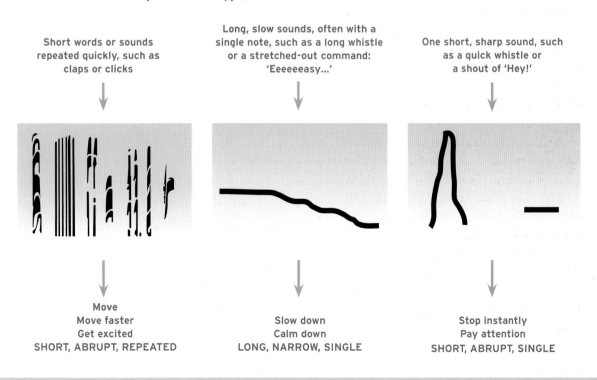

Short words or sounds repeated quickly, such as claps or clicks

Long, slow sounds, often with a single note, such as a long whistle or a stretched-out command: 'Eeeeeeasy...'

One short, sharp sound, such as a quick whistle or a shout of 'Hey!'

Move
Move faster
Get excited
SHORT, ABRUPT, REPEATED

Slow down
Calm down
LONG, NARROW, SINGLE

Stop instantly
Pay attention
SHORT, ABRUPT, SINGLE

In touch with your world

Tactile communication (touch) starts from your earliest moments, when you feel what is going on around you, even before your eyes and ear canals open. As you begin to grow, you may find that you enjoy some areas of your body being touched, while others make you feel uncomfortable.

Every dog is different in how much it likes to be touched. However, newborn puppies, which are blind and deaf, instinctively snuggle in to their mother and siblings, searching out her touch. Dogs and wolves both instinctively seek touch, which may be used to indicate play, friendship, or animosity, and may be demonstrated through pushing, pinning down or biting.

Sensitivity to tactile stimuli varies with context, so your response to touch is likely to reflect a past experience or how you are feeling at a given moment. If you feel relaxed or confident, being touched may not bother you. If you are uncomfortable, perhaps through illness or uncertainty, you will feel more sensitive and may try to move away.

An open mouth is often a sign of relaxation and may indicate that a dog is happy with human touch.

Physical response

As you receive touch, either from a living being or the environment in general, kinesthetic (touch sensory) information travels up to your brain through extension and contraction of your muscles, tendons and joints, and along the nerves, to give you exact information about where you are and in which direction you are moving.

You are sensitive to changes in temperature and pressure, and are most likely to enjoy steady strokes from a firm hand. A light human touch may be interpreted as annoying or exciting, while a heavy hand is likely to feel unpleasant. But every dog feels touch differently, and a pat that is experienced as a gentle reassurance by one dog may be painful to another. Your owner may hug and stroke you, which you may accept and enjoy because of the oxytocin release that results (see pages 150–51). If you have not regularly met new people, however, you may shy away from such advances. Ironically, when dogs indicate their discomfort in this way, it is common for humans to persist, attempting to 'show' the dog that they mean no harm. However, such human signs of affection may be seen as overt threat, particularly if the dog has not been well socialized.

Your owner is likely to be familiar with the 'scratch reflex', which means that when they touch your belly, flanks or back (the 'saddle' region), their touch stimulates nerves under your skin that are connected to the spinal cord. This in turn causes your hind leg to lift and scratch rhythmically. It is an involuntary response, which may explain your puzzled expression when this occurs.

KINESTHETIC SENSORY SYSTEMS

As you move around in your environment, your body picks up information from your kinesthetic (touch sensory) systems, such as those located in your paws and skin, to give you vital information about what is going on around you.

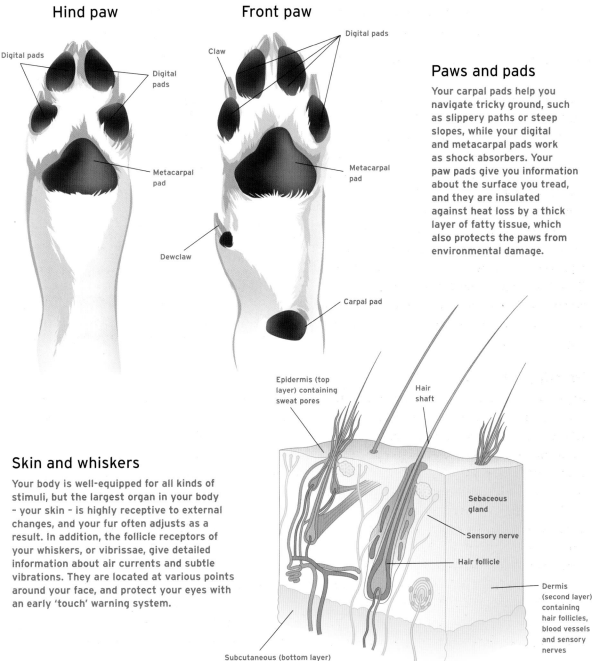

Hind paw

Digital pads

Digital pads

Metacarpal pad

Front paw

Claw

Digital pads

Metacarpal pad

Dewclaw

Carpal pad

Paws and pads

Your carpal pads help you navigate tricky ground, such as slippery paths or steep slopes, while your digital and metacarpal pads work as shock absorbers. Your paw pads give you information about the surface you tread, and they are insulated against heat loss by a thick layer of fatty tissue, which also protects the paws from environmental damage.

Epidermis (top layer) containing sweat pores

Hair shaft

Sebaceous gland

Sensory nerve

Hair follicle

Dermis (second layer) containing hair follicles, blood vessels and sensory nerves

Subcutaneous (bottom layer) containing fat and muscle

Skin and whiskers

Your body is well-equipped for all kinds of stimuli, but the largest organ in your body - your skin - is highly receptive to external changes, and your fur often adjusts as a result. In addition, the follicle receptors of your whiskers, or vibrissae, give detailed information about air currents and subtle vibrations. They are located at various points around your face, and protect your eyes with an early 'touch' warning system.

4
STIMULI AND RESPONSES

Your surroundings will always have an impact on you, from something as large as a change in the climate causing you to feel cold, to a flea hopping across your fur. You experience these changes as stimuli and they trigger a response in you.

Physical responses

You have evolved to react to your ever-changing environment, through actions great and small. Feeling cold may cause you to seek shelter; a fly on your nose might cause you to scratch. Stimulus–response relationships tell us much about how animals have evolved through adapting and reacting.

The stimulus–response mechanism is a vital part of any animal's survival system: any dog that does not respond to a stimulus will not survive for long. Some of these stimulus–response relationships are natural (such as eyes dilating in dark conditions), while some are learned (such as not eating food that once made you sick). These reactions act to keep you safe from harm.

Essentially, touch–response is clear and simple: receptors on your skin respond to a stimulus, such as a stroke from a warm hand, and send impulses along sensory neurons to the central nervous system (CNS). When your owner scratches your head, for instance, receptors in your skin react to the area of touch, the temperature and how much pressure your owner is applying. Your other senses work in similar ways. Chemical receptors in your nose, for example, respond to a broad range of scent and other detectable information such as pheromones.

Instinctive responses

As a dog, you might indicate stimulus–response (SR) patterns that are common to your species. A fast-running rabbit may trigger your chase response, as the cell arrangement in the eyes of some breeds provides a ready mechanism. Species-specific SR relationships may also occur in the social environment. When compared to wolf pups, young dogs aged up to five weeks were seen to show an increased readiness to communicate with their human caregivers and exhibited more signals of distress at separation, wagging their tails and gazing at the human's face. The wolf pups showed more avoidance and even demonstrated some aggressive behaviour towards a familiar person. As all the pups were hand-raised under similar conditions, their differing responses to the same human stimuli are notable.

This behaviour supports the theory that dogs have evolved in partnership with humans. It could be that your innate behaviour focuses on seeking a response from your owner. Observations of SR in dogs has provided us with the canine ethogram: a list of all the various types of behaviour or activity seen in the many different breeds. It can be used to find descriptions of species-specific responses.

When you scratch in response to an itch, you are demonstrating the stimulus-response system in action.

ANATOMY OF THE EYE

Dogs are crepuscular, meaning they like to hunt in the dim light conditions of dawn and dusk, and their eyes (along with most domestic animals) have a special layer of tissue behind the retina that increases the light available to the photoreceptors.

Undilated pupil

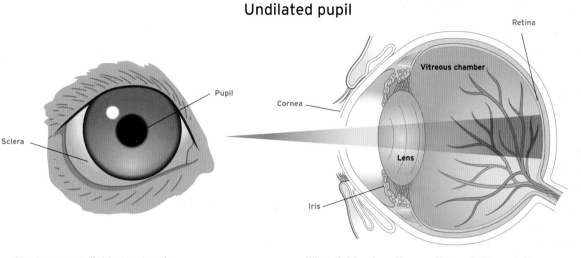

You have more light receptors in your eye than a human does, a larger cornea and a larger pupil, which allows more light to enter the eye.

When light enters the eye, it travels through the lens and onto the retina. In bright light conditions the pupil is undilated; it shrinks to avoid damage to the cornea.

Dilated pupil

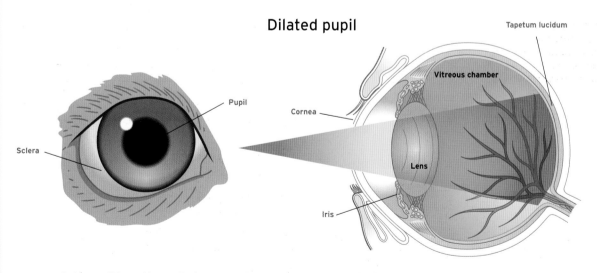

In low light conditions, the pupil dilates to allow more light to enter the eye.

The pupil dilates to allow you to see in dim light conditions. A layer behind the retina called the tapetum reflects the light onto the retina a second time, increasing your ability to see in dim light.

How you learn

From the moment you enter the world, and perhaps even before this, you are aware of your environment and begin to link your responses to certain events. If you hear a loud noise, you startle and may bark. If you smell something tasty, such as your owner's dinner, your mouth may water.

Knee-jerk responses such as salivating over food are simple, instinctive reactions. They are said to be 'hard-wired' in the brain and are produced by a neural pathway or innate releasing mechanism. However, these responses can also be triggered by controlled events and paired with new triggers. In other words, they can be produced in you by humans wanting to teach you new ways of reacting to things.

In the early 20th century, the Russian physiologist Ivan Pavlov performed experiments on dogs that proved he could create new triggers for old responses. While doing research on salivation in dogs, he noticed that they salivated when food was produced. But before long, their salivation response began to occur when the experimenters entered the testing area – before any food was visible. Somehow, their entry had become a trigger for the salivation response. Pavlov hypothesized that the dogs had formed a crucial link between the experimenters' arrival and the meat powder that they always presented during the salivation experiment.

Scientists began to use the term 'unconditioned stimulus' to refer to an event that causes a response to occur, and 'unconditioned response' to describe that natural response or reflex. For any new stimulus that became linked to the original stimulus–response through training, they used the term 'conditioned stimulus'. The conditioned stimulus that the dogs first learned through natural linking was the experimenters' entry.

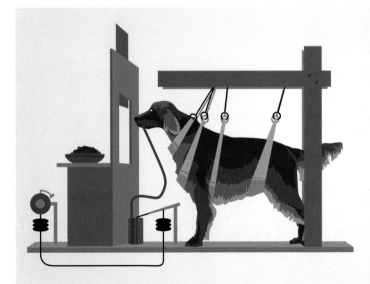

Pavlovian conditioning

Pavlov tested his theory by giving a series of dogs some food at the same time as a metronome made a sound. Initially, the dogs salivated when the food appeared and metronome sounded, and this allowed the dog to pair the conditioned response (salivating) to the sound of the metronome. After repeating the procedure several times, the sound alone caused the dogs to salivate. Pavlov had created a new conditioned response (salivating to the sound of a metronome). This introduction of a linked stimulus became known as a learned or conditioned signal.

Daily learning

Pavlov's conditioned learning theory can be really useful in helping your owner to understand some of the ways that you react to your environment. For instance, you may once have become anxious during a car journey, and displayed physiological signs such as increased heart rate or nausea. On occasions since then, the noise of the car engine may have been enough to trigger this same anxiety, even when the car is still stationary. Further anxiety-provoking journeys may see you start to shiver in anticipatory anxiety as your owner picks up the car keys.

Your owner may sometimes inadvertently cause a new conditioned response. For instance, when you see another dog during a walk, you may become excited, and your owner may pull your lead to bring you closer to them. The tight feeling around your neck may cause discomfort and anxiety. Next time you see another dog, that feeling of anxiety may reappear.

CONDITIONING A RESPONSE

At first

The dog has no particular response to the ticking metronome; there is no link formed. Depending on the individual dog, the sound may elicit a bark, a tentative paw, or no response at all.

A ticking metronome is presented to the dog

During training

By presenting meat with the metronome over a repeated number of occasions, the salivation response that naturally occurs to the meat becomes paired with the metronome too.

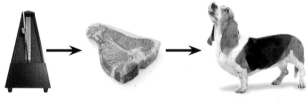

A ticking metronome is presented to the dog along with a piece of meat that causes salivation

Conditioned

Once the conditioned response has been firmly installed, it is possible to present either of the stimuli (the meat or the metronome) and receive the salivation response.

Once the metronome has been linked to the steak, it produces salivation without meat present

When produced alone, the meat continues to produce the natural response of salivation

Learning is rewarding

You are good at learning from the consequences of your actions. If your owner throws a ball for you, you will enjoy running to get it, but unless you bring it back, you cannot continue the game. This consequence will initiate your behaviour of fetching it, rewarding you with the fun of chasing it again.

It is natural for all animals to change what they do in response to the things that happen around them. It is a sign of your intelligence that you learn to stop doing something dangerous or painful, while you also take an increasing part in activities that result in a pleasant or profitable outcome. Emotional responses such as fear, hunger or disgust act to alert animals (including humans) that their safety is at risk; the animal will then take action, if possible, to change the situation. All animals strive to exist in a state of 'homeostasis', or psychological and physical balance, and if they feel they have moved away from this towards an unbalanced state (such as fear, hunger or disgust), they will do whatever seems necessary to return to the equilibrium of homeostasis.

Cause and effect

Thorndike's Law of Effect describes your ability to associate results with actions. In 1898, an American psychologist named Edward Thorndike studied cats' and dogs' abilities to escape from specially designed boxes, which could only be opened by moving a series of latches and pulleys. Food was placed outside the box. Eventually, the hungry animal would trigger the correct latch with which to exit the box and reach the food. The animal was then returned to the box and the time taken to escape was measured once again.

Initially, the latches were opened using trial and error as the animal attempted to exit. After several attempts the animals were quicker to escape because they recalled the method they had previously used.

The food they received (a reward) appeared to motivate them to repeat the learned behaviour. Thorndike concluded that any behaviour that is followed by pleasant consequences is likely to be repeated, while any behaviour that is followed by unpleasant consequences is likely to stop. This led to a new way of understanding how animals could be trained.

Complex learning

Thorndike's research shows two things. First, that you are motivated to respond to your surroundings (such as wanting to escape confinement and also wanting to reach food). Second, it shows that you are capable of remembering how you achieved this – what led to you getting your reward. Even as tasks become more complex, you are able to link the events together and recall the results from your earlier attempts.

You will naturally repeat any actions or activities that are fun or have pleasant consequences.

LEARNING BY REWARD

Thorndike's experiments with cats and dogs proved his Law of Effect: actions that produce rewards tend to be repeated. This explains why you respond so well to positive and motivational training, which increases good behaviour.

Solving the puzzle

Thorndike placed animals inside special puzzle boxes that had a variety of levers and strings inside. Some of these opened the wall of the box when activated, allowing the animal to escape from the box – this was the behaviour that Thorndike wanted the animal to learn.

The door will be released after the dog has pulled on the string

String hangs down inside the box

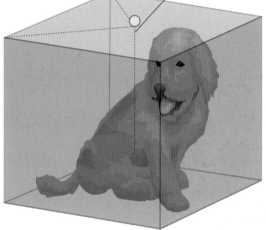

Connected learning

Once free of the box, the animal could access the food that had helped motivate it to find a way out, but now acted also as a reward. Thorndike concluded that all successful behaviours are 'stamped in', while unsuccessful behaviours are 'stamped out'. He also suggested that a response became linked to the associated stimuli by 'stamping in'.

Why did you do that?

As your experience influences how you behave in the future, scientists have experimented with ways they can affect your choices. All learned behaviours – from helping humans as a working dog to navigating jumps with your owner for fun – can result from motivation.

Modern dog training mostly involves 'positive reinforcement' (sometimes also called 'reward-based training') as this is deemed to be the most welfare-friendly approach. It relies on scientific research carried out by American psychologist B.F. Skinner, which built on Thorndike's work to demonstrate the effect of positive and negative consequences on behaviour.

Skinner initially researched the responses of rats and pigeons by placing them in special boxes. In one, the animal would occasionally and accidentally press a lever, at which point a pellet of food appeared. The animal quickly learned to press the lever to obtain food. In a second box, Skinner ran an unpleasant electric current through the floor. The rat found that by pressing a lever (that it first found accidentally), the electric current

would stop. The rats soon learned to go straight to the lever when put in the box. This historical approach strongly influences how you are taught today.

Skinner named this form of learning 'operant conditioning' to reflect how the behaviour 'operates on' or changes the environment (pressing the lever made food appear or pain stop). It is controlled through the use of rewards or punishment. As a consequence, we understand that an animal's choices can be influenced by adding or taking away something they enjoy (reinforcement), or adding or removing something they find unpleasant or aversive (punishment). The consequences are referred to as positive or negative reinforcement, and positive or negative punishment.

Tailored rewards

In order to teach you something in a humane way, your owner needs to use a reward-based system of learning. This means first learning what kind of things you enjoy the most, because these will be used as rewards (positive reinforcement) to influence your choice of behaviour towards your owner's preferred option. Some dogs love furry toys, others like moving ones, and some like a particular kind of food above all else. Your owner can check what works best by examining your responses to what they offer and noticing which reinforcer produces the best results, then tailoring the amounts. It is similar to a person receiving wages: your owner must work out where your minimum and maximum 'wage' levels lie, but in terms of your favoured reward.

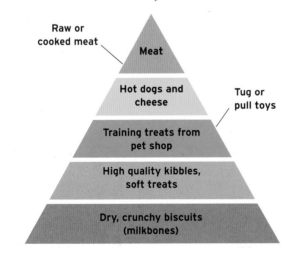

Raw or cooked meat — Meat

Hot dogs and cheese — Tug or pull toys

Training treats from pet shop

High quality kibbles, soft treats

Dry, crunchy biscuits (milkbones)

Every dog has different tastes and preferences, so your owner will need to work out your personal reward scale.

CHANGING BEHAVIOUR

The best way to train you is to reinforce (increase) your good behaviour,
while diminishing any negative behaviour that arises. Learning is divided into
four types of consequence, as shown below.

Positive reinforcement (R+)

Humans can increase positive behaviour by adding things that
a dog likes when the desired behaviour arises. For instance, if
a dog walks well on a long leash, his owner may give him treats
and keep walking forward while the leash is loose.

Positive punishment (P+)

When a negative behaviour arises, an owner may choose to
respond in a way that is experienced as negative by the dog,
such as giving a leash correction if the dog pulls away, and
perhaps verbally scolding him.

Negative reinforcement (R−)

This form of training seeks to increase and encourage good
behaviour by delaying human behaviour that the dog dislikes.
For example, while on a walk, the owner may scold the dog for
pulling. When the dog does not pull, the owner stops scolding.

Negative punishment (P−)

This form of training means delaying things that the dog enjoys
in response to unwanted behaviour, so that the dog will realize
he has to change his behaviour to make the 'good stuff' start
again. For instance, if a dog pulls on the lead while walking, the
owner may stop until the leash becomes loose once more.

Working in partnership

You have a long history of being used for your hunting skills, but it does not explain why you might want to assist people. The recent discovery of large numbers of mammoth remains have led to the hypothesis that you assisted humans in catching such huge numbers of mighty, ancient beasts.

If you are a gundog, you have specific tasks when working with your human handlers. You may be used first to hunt and then to indicate to your human companions where the prey is located by freezing, often in a crouch or 'point' position. When asked, you flush game out without grabbing it for yourself, note where it falls when shot, and then pick it up and deliver it to the arms of your handler. Remarkably, you will also 'honour' another dog's retrieve by not attempting to compete with it for the fallen game that it is seeking.

It seems remarkable that you can be trained to chase across a field (triggered by the natural urge to chase) but then return when asked, or to give up a possible food source that you find extremely tempting, just because you have been ordered to do so. Your ability to be trained in this way is testament to the co-evolution of your intelligence with humans – you willingly allow yourself to be trained by them and work in partnership.

Depending on humans

Humans have long needed your help in hunting for food, but do you need them? While many dogs do live successfully as strays, these 'village dogs' inhabit the periphery of human settlements, surviving by taking food waste that humans leave behind. This is a more uncertain and risky way of living than in human companionship, where you and your puppies are given shelter, food and healthcare. Perhaps the need for safety and survival (for both humans and dogs) lies behind the development of this mutually beneficial relationship.

The Premack Principle

First described by American psychologist David Premack in the 1950s, the Premack Principle states that animals (including humans) will choose to do something they do not wish to do if they believe that they will gain something of greater value (such as 'if you eat your broccoli, you can have ice cream'). It is a long-established teaching practice and may explain why you willingly cooperate on certain things. For instance, your owner may teach you that if you wish to eat dinner, you must first fetch her slippers. For this form of training to be successful, your owner must work out the order in which you value things, so as to be able to play one off against the other.

The gundog's willingness to retrieve and return an item to its owner reflects the value it places on companionship.

USING THE PREMACK PRINCIPLE

First   Then

LEARN TO PLEASE
You need to learn that certain behaviours can bring good outcomes. This link can be discovered by accident or pre-trained. By bringing slippers, this dog earns a meal. The dog also learns that chewing slippers is not as profitable as bringing them to his owner.

SOCIABLE COMPANION
Although people may complain when you jump up at them, you are only trying to earn their attention. Attention is highly reinforcing to a sociable canine. This dog learns to sit in order to earn the enjoyable greeting with his owner.

THE RULES OF PLAY
If you are allowed to drag your owner to the park and then find yourself let off the lead to play freely with other dogs, you will learn that dragging results in play. Your owner needs to teach you to walk next to them, patiently, then reward you with play (the valuable outcome).

REPEAT ENJOYMENT
You can quickly learn to bring back a ball so you can chase it again. This form of play can replace unwanted behaviours such as stealing forbidden items or chasing livestock. The outcome of repeat play is achievable as long as you bring the ball back to your owner.

Your memory

Despite your owner's complaint that you don't remember where you dropped your favourite ball, or that you seem to have forgotten their instructions regarding chewing the wooden chair leg, you do, in fact, have an accomplished memory.

It is commonly said that dogs only 'live in the now'. However, while you experience the world in any given moment much as humans do, you also show the ability to predict future scenarios. This means that you must be remembering things, because it is a memory of feeling nauseous in a car, for example, that makes you feel anxious about travelling next time. Memory is essential for survival and for learning by forming links. But your memory is limited: you remember what is relevant to your wellbeing and survival.

Short- and long-term memory

Your memory is at its best when you are recalling people and places that are linked to safety and survival. A comparison of different species using an elaborate

You can memorize the position of items when hidden, but this memory decays rapidly if the items are not significant to you.

comparison of tests showed that animals, including pigeons, dolphins, rats and dogs, have some form of short-term memory as well as more specialized long-term memories. Memories that contribute to survival are encoded into long-term memory, while the position of a thrown ball might sit temporarily in short-term memory. Dogs form important, life-enhancing social relationships with humans, so those particular humans are significant and their images will be stored in long-term memory. Your attachment to these people also shows how repeated experience creates a powerful memory.

Associative memory

When no important associations are made in any time or place, your memory is quite short; it is believed to be less than two minutes. If you were to toilet in the house, for example, you would not make a specific association with humans disliking the activity unless they happened to catch you in the act and scold you in some way. If they returned at a later time and were angry, you would not be able to link one event to the other, and so would not remember what they had been so cross about.

Scientific experiments suggest that dogs can remember items presented to them for a short time (see opposite), but their performance on this task decayed rapidly. This short-term memory is thought to be very different in context from a memory that may contribute to survival or food location. Wild birds, for instance, remember where they cached valuable sources of food based on how perishable the items are.

DELAYED MATCHING TO SAMPLE TEST

This kind of test demonstrates an animal's working memory: its capability
for remembering things in the short term.

The dog is shown a stimulus,
such as a black triangular toy.

The stimulus is then removed.

After a while, the dog is presented
with the original stimulus plus a
new one (such as a circular toy)
and allowed to choose one of them.

If the dog remembers and chooses
the original stimulus (the triangular
toy) he receives a reward.

What are humans saying?

When people are training you, it looks as though you are learning lots of words, especially those that are linked to actions that your owner wishes you to perform. You can also be trained to respond to other sounds and signals known as 'cues'. But how much do you really understand?

Commonly, whistles are used as signals for sheep dogs and gundogs, but any sound can be linked with desired actions. Your owner may teach you, for example, that the word sound 'Sit!' means 'place your rear end on the floor in the hope of a treat', or that 'Down!' means 'lie on the ground'.

Variations in cue sounds

Cultural and historical differences may result in cue words varying. For instance, trainers in the UK have traditionally said 'Heel!' or 'Close!' when they want you to walk close to them, while in other countries the instruction is 'Hip!'. If you have been taught that a cue links to a particular response, you do not mind what the cue sounds like as long as a reward is offered when you produce the desired behaviour.

Humans sometimes make variations in these cue sounds; their tone of voice or the word itself may sometimes change. This is confusing for you. 'Sit!' and 'Sit down!' are not quite the same, and you may be unable to produce the required behaviour. You associate cue words with both behaviours and consequences, such

Can you understand human conversation?

'Max, teddy - fetch!'

As your owner chats away to you, do you follow each word? Humans often overestimate what you understand when they speak. It is likely you are reading emotions from the sounds they are making, associating their expression and body language with the noises you hear. Without an association being formed between a word and an action in the past, you will simply look for other signals of meaning. To give you a clear understanding of the words your owner uses, they must first teach you just as carefully and thoroughly as Rico and Chaser were taught.

as rewards or punishment. This is why you are likely to refuse to return to your owner when hearing the cue 'Come!' if the last time you did this your owner put you on the lead and took you away from the park where you were happily playing. 'Come!' has now come to mean not just 'return to your owner' but also 'it's the end of the game'.

Understanding names

Your owner may have taught you many cue words, but are you interpreting their requirements by just the words themselves, or are you reading human body signals and making inferences from the context? Is verbal understanding possible in animals that cannot themselves speak?

Research suggests that dogs can be taught to recognize a vast number of cues and to link words with objects. In 2004, Juliane Kaminski and colleagues at the Max-Planck Institute for Evolutionary Anthropology, Germany, set up an experiment in which Rico, a Border Collie, was asked to match an object to a name given by his owner. Rico understood over 200 words, could match

them to objects, fetch named toys from a selection of toys and even recall them four weeks later.

It was suggested that Rico could learn words for new objects by a psychological process known as 'fast mapping', a process that children use to form assumptions about the name of an object based on a single exposure. This may have been due to Rico's ability to recognize the difference between familiar and unfamiliar items. It was suggested he could spot the 'new' word or object and would link it to the new item.

Other dogs have since shown a similar ability – most notably Chaser, a Border Collie owned by John Pilley, Professor of Psychology in South Carolina, USA. Chaser was able to recognize the names of 1,022 objects. The researchers suggested that they might have been able to teach her to learn more, were it not for time constraints, and that the dog remembered more object names than they themselves were able to do. This research shows that, as a dog, you can discriminate objects visually, remember all their names, and map the two together to a remarkable degree.

During the Chaser experiments, the Collie was tested on her ability to match names and objects, and to distinguish 'category' words. She was able to understand the word 'toy' as referring to all 1,022 items, as well as other names (such as 'ball') that referred to an item type. In 2013, Chaser was further able to demonstrate an ability to follow human syntax; she could follow a preposition, such as 'to' or 'in'; a verb such as 'take', and the name of the object. So, for example she could follow specific details such as: 'To ball, take Frisbee'.

Timing is everything

Dogs are skilled at changing their behaviour to fit their environment, which includes their owner. Humans sometimes compare dogs from one family to the next, wondering why they are so different. The answer is that each dog changes their behaviour to meet the needs of their household.

You are aware that one thing leads to another, which means that people can teach you things using stimulus and response techniques. However, if an event is too distant in time or situation from another, no learning takes place. This is because the stimulus–response relationship has to be 'contiguous'; the two things must happen very close together for you to determine a link.

You can only learn when your owner is able to provide you with clear links between actions and consequences.

You also need to be able to see that one event causes another. This is known as 'contingency'. The laws of cause and effect exist whether you notice them or not, but for you to learn about your environment you need to notice that there are consequences to your own or others' actions. You do not always have control over what happens to you, but you can link and learn when things change. How you respond to change can be significant in how you manage, or even survive, in the future.

This type of learning is likely to appear in your everyday life. For instance, if someone places a stairgate across a doorway to prevent you running out of the house, they have changed your surroundings both contingently and contiguously. The gate is there at the moment you try to run (contiguous) and when the gate is closed you cannot exit (contingent).

Conversely, if you have toileted indoors earlier in the day and your human discovers it long after the deed is done, punishing you for this event at that much later time is ineffective. Even if you can still see the patch of urine, you will not link this with the urge to toilet that arose several hours ago. If the human had managed to interrupt you mid-stream and redirected you outside, then rewarded you for completing the act in the correct place, you would remember to do this again, as the reward is contingent on the act of urination and happens immediately afterwards. Any reaction that follows long after the event simply has no effect and could be considered cruel or at best unfair, as you will have no link to follow to the original cause of that reaction.

CONTINGENCY/CONTIGUITY MAP

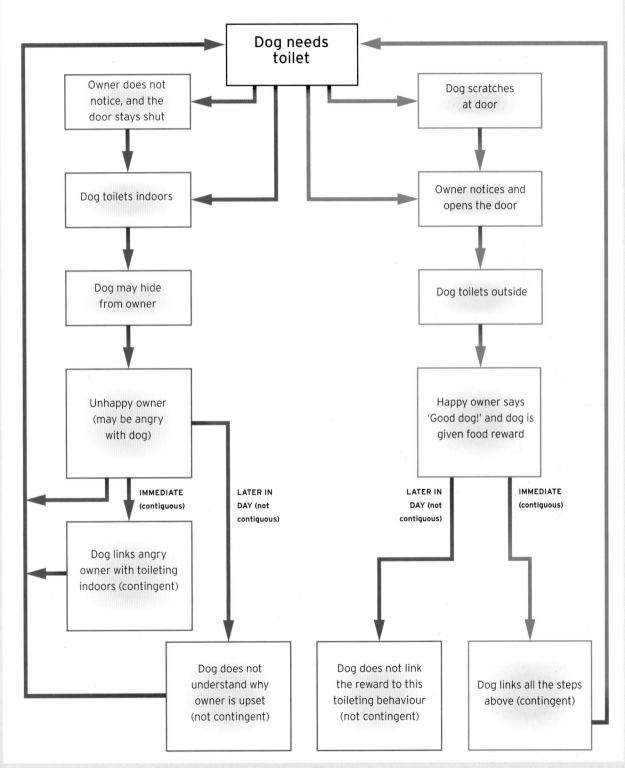

Sixth sense

Can you understand your owner's intention to take you to the vet or out for a walk before they have done anything to indicate this? It seems that a skill known as 'associative learning' helps you predict future events from past experience and act in line with these predictions.

When you witness an event, you may or may not attach significance to it. If the event is salient to you – such as a perceived threat or treat – you may strongly remember the exact situation in which the event occurred, and be able to recall it in future. You will remember what it is you did, who else was there and when it happened – and may even attempt to work out why it occurred. All of these are part of a natural behavioural response to a significant stimulus. During the process, you will also notice and associate other stimuli in the surroundings, along with

the important event. Some of these may not be relevant, but you will link them to the outcome, and so they will be part of the learning you take away from the event.

Environmental cues

You will learn to link regular events, which may not be directly relevant to the main event, but which serve as a good predictor. For example, your owner may come home at the same time of day as lots of other people. The increase in the traffic passing near your home may be a link that you form to predict that your owner will soon appear. Even if you cannot see the vehicles, you may be able to hear them or feel the rumbling as they pass.

Your sensitivity to your environment, along with your acute senses, may lead humans to believe you have a supernatural ability. Animals have been witnessed to flee ahead of natural disasters such as tsunamis and earthquakes, and so they have been studied in China to attempt prediction of such events, with varying success. Early records from Ancient Greece in 373 BCE by the historian Diodorus Siculus describes rats, weasels and snakes fleeing the city of Helice before an earthquake.

It is thought that animals may be aware of 'foreshocks' that humans do not register, or other environmental changes such as the trembling soundwaves that precede thunder. The series of electrical discharges resulting from atmospheric conditions during a thunderstorm, being relatively uncommon, may result in your feeling uncertain or uncomfortable (a response that in turn may be noticed by your owners).

Your heightened sensitivity, especially to sound, means you may perceive things that your owner cannot.

ASSOCIATING EVENTS

Over time, you will begin to link certain things that your owner does with events that you like or dislike. For instance, if your owner picks up the house keys and your lead, you will anticipate going out for a walk. Other examples are shown below.

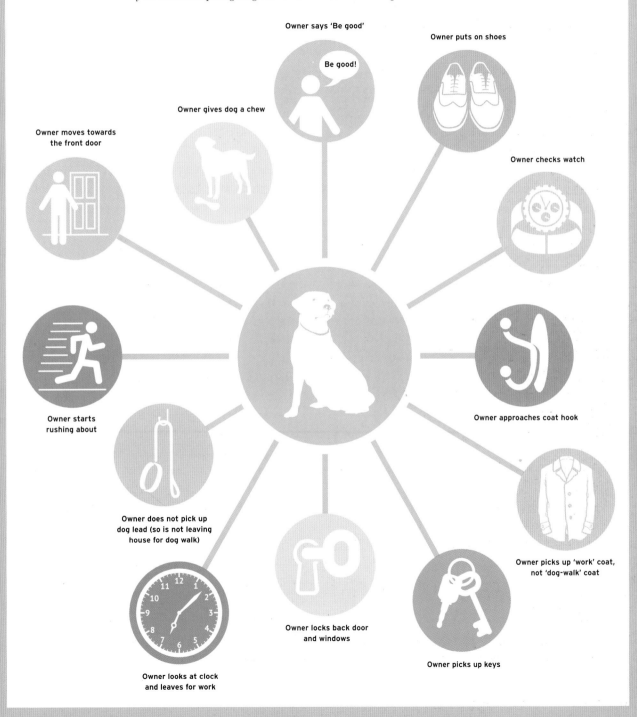

Owner says 'Be good'

Owner puts on shoes

Owner gives dog a chew

Owner moves towards the front door

Owner checks watch

Owner starts rushing about

Owner approaches coat hook

Owner does not pick up dog lead (so is not leaving house for dog walk)

Owner picks up 'work' coat, not 'dog-walk' coat

Owner looks at clock and leaves for work

Owner locks back door and windows

Owner picks up keys

Sensitization and phobias

You will notice anything that might cause a problem so that you can protect yourself from harm. Part of your survival system includes the phenomenon of 'stimulus generalization', which allows you to remember not only the main part of a frightening event, but also anything associated with it.

The psychological process of stimulus generalization explains how you can become reactive to many different things after experiencing an extreme fear reaction in a particular instance. In addition, if the scary situation happens repeatedly and you are unable to cope, your response amplifies. In other words, you become more sensitized to that situation.

One-trial learning

In the 1930s, US philosopher and psychologist Edwin Guthrie carried out experiments to prove that one significant event (or single exposure) was enough to provide an animal with response behaviours that would repeatedly occur. This means that if your last trip in the car led to a painful vet visit, you may remember everything that led up to it, including the car journey, getting into the car, leaving the house and even your owner putting on their shoes in readiness. This anxiety-linked associative learning means that next time your owner reaches for their shoes, you may run away.

Developing a phobia

You may be naturally sensitive to loud noises, but imagine that one evening, while you are out for a walk with your owner, a series of loud explosions startles you and causes you to race for home, pulling your owner behind you. When safely indoors, you dive for cover under your owner's bed. The next time your owner wishes to take you out for your walk, you refuse to leave the house in anticipation that the loud noises, which you do not know

were just a firework display, will recur. You begin hiding under the bed more frequently to avoid what you see as a future threat. If your owner attempts to coax or pull you out from your safe place, you behave aggressively, forcing them to leave you in peace. If they do move you, you may then learn to defend yourself more vigorously when they attempt to reach towards you in future, even if this is only a hand reaching out to pet you. In this way, a single incident that caused a fear response can ripple across multiple incidents, in each of which you feel that your safety is compromised. This is how phobias develop.

You may develop a fear of getting into a car if you have experienced a frightening event after one such trip.

THE FEAR RESPONSE

When you experience an event as fearful, your body will involuntarily display certain physiological changes, which will include some or all of those shown below.

- Self-directed chewing (paws, flanks)
- Shaking
- Rapid panting
- Hiding
- Drooling
- Pacing
- Freezing
- Escape/bolting
- Aggression
- Scanning/hypervigilance

These responses are related to your experience of possible threat or perceived danger and are not as simplistic as the description 'fight or flight' might sound. You may show other avoidance signals that develop more slowly as you take in information.

Developing habits

A 'habit' refers to a regular tendency – often one that is hard to give up. Every dog (and human) can form habits, which may occur as a result of linking multiple situations and outcomes. Due to the enormous variation of personal experience, your habits reflect your individuality.

All of your experiences have added to your learning. Significant and repeated experiences will inform you about how to react to events like those in the future.

Your owner began learning how to write words by mastering the alphabet, but they learned to speak by listening to people speaking around them. This type of learning occurs from an early age, well before a child can form words. What the child hears are sounds, which begin to have meanings and can ultimately be recognized as grouped into complete sentences. These may also have emotional expression attached. When you are at training class for dogs, your learning is arranged in a careful step-by-step manner. However, every other part of your life also teaches you lessons, just as children learn to speak. This 'composite' or blended learning refers to all the influences around you.

Remembering details

When meeting another dog for the first time, you will be aware of their scent, appearance, actions and reactions, who they are with, the weather on that day and the environment in which you meet. If you have eaten something unpleasant earlier, you might be feeling unwell, which will also affect how you experience them. You then store all these details in your memory, because they might assist you in the future. If one instance becomes significant, you generalize these additional details so that the next time you meet a similar looking dog, you expect similar things to occur.

Composite learning

Your owner might not realize it, but they significantly influence the formation of your habits. You are affected by events, but you are also affected by your owner's reaction: if they become upset when you show signs of nervousness, this response provides additional feedback and adds to your composite learning.

Composite learning often lies at the core of behavioural problems. This is reflected in the way that inappropriate behaviours are often habitual and tend to recur under particular circumstances. An animal behaviourist can deconstruct a habit to its component triggers (such as hearing a car horn) to desensitize and counter-condition a dog to more appropriate (and happier) responses. Sometimes an expert will test a dog's response to another dog by using a fake or 'stooge' dog in its place. The visual appearance of the fake dog is often sufficient to trigger the original response, so can be used to provide a mild, then increasing, exposure. Habits can therefore be both made and lost.

IDENTIFYING TRIGGERS

In any situation, a dog's behaviour will reflect his past experience of events, as these may have made him more or less fearful of certain things. If a dog reacts strongly to a particular situation, it is useful to break the situation down into its component triggers and estimate how much each causes a reaction in the dog.

Scenario A

A human adult enters a house quickly and unannounced one evening. The adult is unknown to the dog, but approaches him and tries to stroke him. Although the adult is quiet, the other triggers (strange human and reaching hand) are problematic for this particular dog due to his past experience. Combined, they lead the dog to bite the person.

Triggers and strength of reaction (0 = mild trigger, 10 = extreme trigger)

Low end	Scale (0–10)	High end
Small person		Large person
Gradual		Sudden
Familiar (known to dog)		Unfamiliar (not known to dog)
Quiet		Loud
Daylight		Dusk or dark
Far away		Close up
Keep hands still		Reaches out to dog

Scenario B

Children enter a room where a dog they play with regularly is sitting. The children enter the house after being invited in by the owner and they are told not to try to touch the dog. Although the children are loud (which can trigger defensive behaviour in the dog), all the other factors involved are enjoyable for him, so no problem behaviour occurs.

Triggers and strength of reaction (0 = mild trigger, 10 = extreme trigger)

Low end	Scale (0–10)	High end
Small person		Large person
Gradual		Sudden
Familiar (known to dog)		Unfamiliar (not known to dog)
Quiet		Loud
Daylight		Dusk or dark
Far away		Close up
Keep hands still		Reaches out to dog

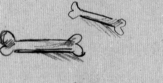

5
PUPPYHOOD

Puppy behaviours tend to be based on early instincts and abilities, but this does not mean that your mind was a 'blank slate' at birth. It is thought that puppies are influenced by their mother's physical and emotional states during pregnancy, and their genetic make-up. But when it comes to learning lessons from the environment, the puppy stage is critical in learning how to interact with the world.

Being a puppy

Puppyhood is a critical stage in your life, because puppies learn rapidly as their bodies and brains develop. As you interact with your parents and littermates, you will roll around, grab with your mouth, chase and hunt. You are rehearsing essential social skills that you will call on all your life.

During the socialization stage (also referred to as the 'sensitive' period) at 3–13 weeks of age, it is very important for you to mix with other dogs and people of all ages and walks of life. The socialization period is a time-critical stage and any breeder or prospective owner must take advantage of this important phase in their puppy's development to teach them well. Failing to do so could cause you irreparable harm (see pages 90–91).

Your new home

You are usually adopted into a human family at some point during the socialization stage. Typically, this occurs at around 6–8 weeks of age, although some experts recommend waiting until the puppy is 10 weeks of age. This stage of life may coincide with a time of increased sensitivity, so it is important that your breeder begins the ongoing social experience that you require and that your new family maintain it too. Going to a new home represents an enormous period of sudden change, requiring you to adjust rapidly to new surroundings and people, while detaching successfully from your previous dog family. No wonder you might react with distress, especially at night (see page 99).

Juvenile stage

The juvenile stage is perhaps the one that most owners recognize. By this point you are making clear learning-based decisions and associating cause and effect based on your experiences. It is a good time to start more formal learning such as puppy classes, as you develop the skills

that assist you in living with humans and others. Your experiences teach you about the world gradually, and should not be seen as final, but it may be harder to change the course of any learning at a later date.

Your emotional responses are expected to depend on your prior experience and can be seen in context (so they will be different for every puppy). Puppies with limited previous experience in terms of people and surroundings (particularly those coming from non-domestic environments or rural surroundings) may not cope well in situations that crop up later in their lives, such as veterinary examinations.

Your experiences as a puppy will influence how you see the world and its events throughout adulthood too.

SIGNIFICANT LIFE STAGES

Your development is viewed from the perspective of time-sensitive periods
that will vary from one dog to another. These stages will also overlap and should
be seen as transitionary rather than clearly divided stages (note that all timings
are approximate and may vary from dog to dog).

Prenatal (before birth)
Puppies may be influenced by levels of stress or other conditions in the mother.

Neonatal (birth-2 weeks)
You are heavily dependent on your mother for warmth and food, as well as
her licking you to stimulate elimination. Puppies can learn through touch
and scent. Puppies suckle; if separated from the mother during this stage
can learn to show excessive mouthing behaviour in later life.

Transitional (2-3 weeks)
A period of rapid change, where you become able to stand up,
gradually building up to walking. You start to toilet outside the nest
rather than needing your mother's help. As well as playing with
littermates, you start to growl and your tail gives its first wag. Your
ear canals open at around 18-20 days and you may startle at noises.
Motor systems and sensory systems develop rapidly. Eyes and ear
canals open. At this stage puppies begin to move around more and
may vocalize when separated from litter or mother.

Socialization (3-13 weeks)
Effects of the environment have the greatest influence on
behavioural development at this stage. Emotional attachments
are formed in a social environment and other surroundings.

Juvenile (13 weeks-adult)
Your strength and skill continues to develop, but you must
stay actively within your social environment, or your
confidence could regress. This period lasts until you reach
sexual maturity. Social maturity takes significantly longer,
in some cases perhaps occurring over the course of several
years. (See page 100 for more on the juvenile).

Adulthood (6-18 months onwards, depending on breed)
You continue to learn and explore your world, developing
knowledge about your family and social surroundings.

Mixing with friends

'Socialization' refers to the activity of mixing with all the elements of your environment in a way that you enjoy while you are still a young puppy. This allows you to habituate to everyday occurrences that could otherwise cause stress, especially mixing with humans of all ages and other dogs.

Dogs that have been kept away from an everyday household experience (perhaps kept in kennels or a barn) cannot develop coping mechanisms for this later in life. This means you will not learn how to socialize with others if it did not occur when you were 3–13 weeks old.

The level to which you can socialize as an adult is proportionate to your experience (or lack of it) as a puppy. This is because dogs learn what is 'normal' and unthreatening through a process of 'habituation', whereby events that are routinely experienced during the first three months are downgraded in terms of attention because they have repeatedly been shown to be 'unthreatening' and can safely be ignored. A lack of habituation to socializing with people and other animals may result in fearfulness towards them.

Your effect on humans

As a puppy, you have an appealing appearance, with eyes and ears that look large in proportion to your head. You often attract social attention. This charm is helpful to your owner, who may want you to mix with plenty of humans. It is due to something known as the 'baby schema' effect – your combination of huge eyes, plump face, chubby body and short limbs are designed to promote feelings of care and nurture in your parents and human caretakers, while decreasing any feelings of aggression. A research study in 2012 by Nittono and colleagues at the University of Hiroshima, Japan, found that simply looking at photographs of cute animals and babies was enough to make the viewers not only feel good, but also act in a more physically tender manner.

Socializing with children when you are 3-13 weeks old ensures that you feel secure around people of all ages as you grow older.

LAYERS OF SOCIAL ENVIRONMENT

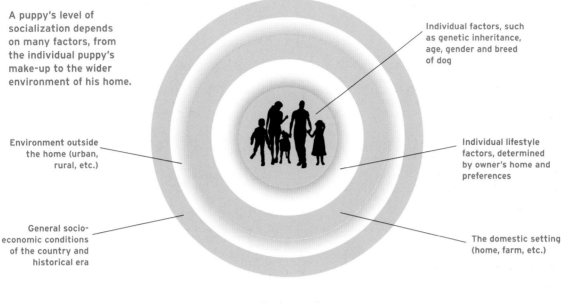

A puppy's level of socialization depends on many factors, from the individual puppy's make-up to the wider environment of his home.

Individual factors, such as genetic inheritance, age, gender and breed of dog

Environment outside the home (urban, rural, etc.)

Individual lifestyle factors, determined by owner's home and preferences

General socio-economic conditions of the country and historical era

The domestic setting (home, farm, etc.)

Baby schema

The key features of the 'baby schema' have been found to release dopamine in the mammalian brain. Scientists think this acts to encourage caretaking behaviour, and so ensure the baby animal's survival.

1 Disproportionately large head
2 Big eyes
3 Round face

4 Chubby cheeks
5 High forehead
6 Short nose (snout)
7 Soft skin (or fur)

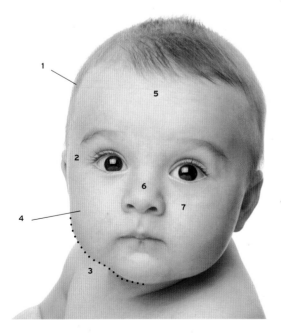

Puppy behaviour tests

Every new owner will want to ensure they choose a puppy suited to their lifestyle, both for your sake and their own. This is because you will become a close member of the family. You can adapt to some extent, but there are overriding factors that influence this process before you even arrive home.

Not all puppies are born alike. Their appearance may be similar, but they will have very different characters.

It is important for your owner to see you with your mother and to establish that she is directly related to the litter of pups. Unscrupulous sellers may attempt to pass off a litter as being from another female dog, and this can have extremely negative results. Research by the Association of Pet Behaviour Counsellors, whose members deal with behaviour problems in family pets, showed that 20 per cent of owners did not see one or both of the puppy's parents. When only one parent was seen with the puppies, owners were two and a half times more likely to visit a pet behaviourist than those who saw both parents. Owners who did not see either of the puppy's parents were four times more likely to seek behavioural help.

Helping the nervous system

Social interaction activates your parasympathetic nervous system, resulting in relaxation and greater emotional attachment later in life. A lack of touch during the prenatal stage and puppyhood, on the other hand, is likely to create real problems for your owner, visitors and any vets that you visit. Research has shown that gently petting ('gentling') the pregnant mother dog during the prenatal stage and then the puppies during the neonatal stage can help puppies to develop resilience to stress later in life, including improving your learning capacity and ability to cope with isolation. Specific methods vary for gentling, but it involves brief periods of massaging, stroking and holding a puppy in ways that do not create alarm but instead allow the animal to enjoy and habituate to interaction with humans.

Military routines

The US military went so far as to develop a 'Bio-Sensor' routine aimed to give animals this early neurological stimulation and an early advantage in life. These exercises were carried out in addition to normal handling and socialization, and were carefully carried out for a very short amount of time (3–5 seconds), once a day, to make sure the neurological system was not over-stimulated, which would have negative and harmful results. The exercises were carried out by experts, and included tickling between the puppy's toes; holding him in an upright (perpendicular) position – head up, then head down; holding the puppy in the palm of the hands, back against the palm; and placing the puppy on a cool, damp towel without restricting his movements.

PUPPY CHOICE GUIDELINES

OBSERVATIONS	HOW TO OBSERVE	WHAT TO LOOK FOR
View the mother and father to assess your puppy's likely future temperament.	Spend time with the puppy's parents.	Friendliness, barking, avoidance nervousness, takes treats nicely.
A breeder will have other relatives, aunts and older half-siblings.	Spend time with older puppy siblings and wider family.	Gets on well with other dogs present. Excitability when together. Do any dogs need to be kept separate?
Puppy health screening	Breeder will have records of this specific to the breed(s) involved.	Signed Veterinary records. Kennel Club certification. Is breeder aware of health issues related to this breed e.g. breathing problems, heart disorders, eye defects?
Male puppy?	Decide on existing dogs in your family (male-female pairs can lead to less conflict). Male hormones can lead to leg-cocking, urination, and risky behaviours in adolescence such as fighting. Risk of roaming looking for females in season.	Breeder can identify the sex of the puppy.
Female puppy?	Decide on existing dogs in your family (male-female pairs can lead to less conflict). Females will come into season, often twice a year. Potential for puppies.	Breeder can identify the sex of the puppy.
Bolder puppy behaviour. (Note: you should meet each puppy at least three times to obtain a fair assessment.)	Take each puppy to a separate area individually and play with them using toys and food the breeder provides.	One that 'chooses you'. Does not let go of toys or treats easily. Does not stop readily when gently dissuaded. Mouths you or clothing persistently. May bark for more attention. Struggles and fights when picked up. (This behaviour may need expert assistance in future.)
Timid puppy behaviour. (Note: you should meet each puppy at least three times to obtain a fair assessment.)	Take each puppy to a separate area individually and play with them using toys and food the breeder provides.	May avoid interaction with you. Will not approach. May sit/freeze. May growl and appear uncertain. May bark when worried or startled. Struggles and fights when picked up. (This behaviour may need expert assistance in future.)
Calm, relaxed puppy behaviour. (Note: you should meet each puppy at least three times to obtain a fair assessment.)	Take each puppy to a separate area individually and play with them using toys and food the breeder provides.	Approaches readily. Plays with 'give and take' to allow you to have toy at times. Moves away from you at times to explore the surroundings. Will mouth and nibble but stops when gently distracted. Relaxes when picked up.
Socialization 'status' (1)	Puppy's existing level of interaction with household environment.	Puppies should be raised within a household, where they have experienced noises from appliances such as fridges and televisions.
Socialization 'status' (2)	Puppy's existing level of interaction with other dogs and people.	Puppies should be raised in a household that includes people of all ages and life stages. Interact with the puppies.
Socialization 'status' (3)	For older puppies (over 12 weeks).	Socialization (1) and (2) must already have taken place, but also car journeys and outside experience. Puppies should have been vaccinated by breeder in order to allow this essential early learning.

Puppy genetics

Looks alone are not a clear guide to how you will develop, and even if your pedigree is registered it may not provide an exact prediction of your growth. While a pedigree records animal descent, the term 'pure-bred' is misleading, as you are all part of the same species: *Canis familiaris*.

DNA profiling (or 'genetic fingerprinting') is a forensic method used to identify individuals through genetic material. DNA profiling is used in the human world mainly to identify criminals or establish familial links, because the chance of two humans having the same DNA (unless they are twins) is one in a billion.

DNA testing

DNA profiling has entered the dog world in several ways. For instance, it can be used to provide evidence of your identity if you are ever stolen or lost. Dog DNA matching has been used in forensic situations to link a victim or perpetrator to a crime scene, which testifies to a

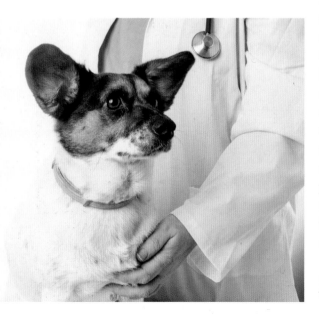

recognition by the legal profession that dog owners live in an environment that is rich with canine material.

More recently, DNA analysis has been used to compare the DNA of a particular dog to a database of listed breeds (though different databases exist according to your country of origin). Your genealogy can be investigated by matching your sample to that of others, looking for similarities and differences in genetic markers. The DNA sample is commonly taken by buccal (cheek) swab, where a soft brush is gently swept inside the dog's cheek. It is a permanent, unchanging record.

Genetically creating health

DNA testing can reveal the presence of genes linked to disease, which is important for both pedigree and cross-breed dogs. A responsible breeder will arrange for tests to be performed on any breeding stock to identify possible genetic defects and results will be openly presented to prospective buyers. However, not all defects are congenital (present at the time of birth) and some may develop later in life. Inherited disorders are described as 'simple' or 'complex'. Simple defects are usually caused by a single gene mutation, and may present as eye problems or deafness. Complex inherited disorders involve several genes as well as environmental factors and may result in problems such as hip and elbow dysplasia, epilepsy or heart disease.

DNA tests are quick and inexpensive. For the dog, they involve no more than a painless cheek swab.

IDENTIFYING ANCESTRY

The ancestral tree

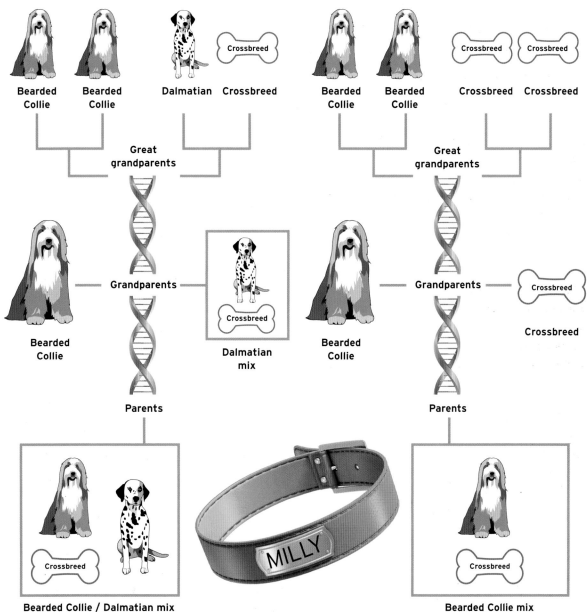

Bearded Collie

Bearded Collie

Dalmatian

Crossbreed

Bearded Collie

Bearded Collie

Crossbreed

Crossbreed

Great grandparents

Great grandparents

Bearded Collie

Crossbreed

Dalmatian mix

Bearded Collie

Crossbreed

Crossbreed

Grandparents

Grandparents

Parents

Parents

Crossbreed

Crossbreed

MILLY

Bearded Collie / Dalmatian mix

Bearded Collie mix

A database of nearly 200 breeds is used to detect possible matches to a dog's DNA sample. An algorithm predicts the most likely combination of pedigree and cross-breed dogs in the subject dog's immediate history. Where a crossbreed is detected, it can be difficult to identify the composite individual breeds accurately. As a result the most statistically likely match is presented. Potential matches are identified indicating the level of likelihood, but it is unlikely that the exact breeds were all present.

Learning good habits

As a puppy, you will not automatically know your owner's rules. At first, you may not be able to navigate up and down stairs, nor have control over your need to toilet. Even when you manage to master these skills, you cannot know what your owner expects of you until you are taught 'good' habits.

Habits that are deemed 'good' tend to be those that suit domestic living, where you live in a home and interact socially with humans, dogs and other species such as cats, rabbits or rats. Some undesirable natural habits, such as puppy biting, may fade with age, but desired responses, such as going outside to toilet, need to be established with training. You cannot learn these alone.

Housetraining habits

In the litter, the mother licks her puppies to encourage them to toilet, then cleans them up. After a while, they may learn to leave their nest and eliminate, returning to the nest immediately afterwards. Depending on the

existing habits of the mother, the pups may not naturally take themselves away further from the nest. Puppies raised in puppy farms are often contained in small areas where the mother herself is unable to leave to toilet away from the nest. If the mother soils the sleeping area, the puppies may learn to accept this as the norm and behave in the same way. This may hinder housetraining once the puppies are in their new home.

The location and the surface you toilet upon as a developing puppy will affect your later behaviour. If you are left to toilet repeatedly in the same area, this will rapidly become your normal choice. Fortunately, your behaviour is reasonably predictable, so your new owner

RISE AND SHINE

Puppies respond well to routine, and it is important to make sure they have plenty of opportunities for rest and sleep, as well as appropriate nourishment and socialization with people and animals.

6-6.30 am	6.30-7 am	7-9 am	9-11 am	11-11.30 am	11.30-12.30 pm
Toilet	Breakfast	Playtime and short walk to socialize	Nap time in crate (may need toilet)	Toilet	Play, toilet then lunch

can monitor your daily timetable and take action. Puppies tend to urinate within 30 seconds of waking and defecate within around two minutes, which gives your owner just enough time to take you straight to a chosen toilet location and then offer you a reward for performing a behaviour that they would like to encourage in you.

Sweet dreams

Newborn puppies sleep in a heap and spend around 96 per cent of their time asleep. During puppyhood, you need to sleep more than the average adult dog, and may even need to sleep for 12–14 hours in every 24-hour cycle. Research suggests that nearly all of your sleep is REM (rapid eye movement) sleep, which is associated with dreaming, but other forms of sleep will develop as you grow: REM sleep drops from 85 per cent at 7 days to 7 per cent at 35 days. By four weeks of age, you will seek to sleep alongside your siblings, instead of on top of them. Your human family must always be prepared to provide you with lots of chances to rest, because otherwise your behaviour is likely to deteriorate through tiredness.

Puppies need training in house-friendly behaviours so that they are compatible with and happy in the family.

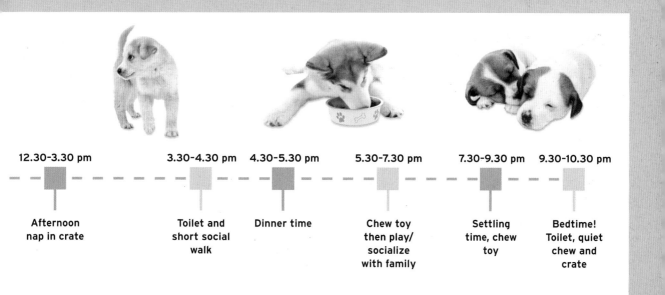

12.30-3.30 pm	3.30-4.30 pm	4.30-5.30 pm	5.30-7.30 pm	7.30-9.30 pm	9.30-10.30 pm
Afternoon nap in crate	Toilet and short social walk	Dinner time	Chew toy then play/ socialize with family	Settling time, chew toy	Bedtime! Toilet, quiet chew and crate

A healthy puppy physical

When you are very young – about 5–9 weeks of age – you will be taken to a vet, who will register you and check your development. He or she will make sure you are happy during your visit, so you do not develop any negative associations to the vets, nurses, clinic, or even its smells and sounds.

At your first visit to a veterinary clinic, you will be given an injection (or more than one) to protect you against the more common, potentially fatal infectious diseases, such as Canine Distemper, Hepatitis, Parvovirus, and Leptospirosis. You will need at least two vaccinations to establish long-term immunity from the diseases, and you may be given vaccinations every 3–4 weeks from 8–17 weeks old.

The vet will educate your owner in all the things that they need to know about your health care, including diseases to watch out for and relevant information about your breed (such as breed-linked health issues). The vet can also tell your owner about the importance of socialization and general training, and help them identify any early problems.

Your owner will learn about regular worming and flea control, nutrition, neutering, dental care and microchipping (which is now compulsory in some countries). They also need to learn how to take care of your skin and coat, to monitor possible problems with your anal glands and to remain vigilant about checking your ears for any infection, dirt or blockage. Regular visits to your vet practice will help you habituate the experience (see pages 80–83) and adapt to any form of treatment without developing fear.

Social and healthy

During the socialization period (3–13 weeks) you must experience what life has to offer, especially in terms of company, while avoiding sources of infection. As a puppy, you may be invited to puppy sessions where you can play with other young puppies until your vaccination course is complete and you can venture outdoors. This gives you a chance to socialize without putting your health at risk. Your behaviour and body language must be carefully monitored as you interact. If you are nervous or reluctant to engage, even after a period of gentle encouragement, you may need help from a behaviour specialist, who can suggest some easy confidence-building exercises. This early intervention will help you from developing a long-term fearful response. On the other hand, if you are behaving roughly or not taking into account the responses of the puppies you are playing with, a behaviourist can show your owner how to introduce you gently while you learn essential impulse control.

Puppies are typically vaccinated for the first time at 8-10 weeks and will need a course of vaccinations.

INTERNAL AND EXTERNAL PARASITES

Most dogs will suffer from an invasion of parasites at one time or another, so it is important to have regular checks by your owner and vet. Parasites can begin by causing irritation but may progress to life-threatening conditions if untreated.

Fleas – these small insects prefer warmth and are rife in the summer months when they can pass between animals. Scratching is the main symptom.

Flea

Worms – such as roundworms, hookworms, whipworms and tapeworms. Symptoms include diarrhoea, weight loss, deterioration of appearance and sometimes vomiting.

Tapeworm

Ear mite

Ear mites – these small parasites pass between animals and can spread to other parts of the body. Symptoms include itching of the ears, head and neck, scratching around the head, frequently shaking the head. Red-brown crusts may appear on the outer ear.

Tick

Ticks – these parasites attach themselves by mouth to the skin of dogs and feed on their blood. They can cause disease and anaemia. Ticks are visibly present on the skin, especially as they enlarge with blood.

Where you need guidance

When you are young, your environment is new and exciting, and you learn about it rapidly through interacting with it. You scratch, scrape, chase and pounce, and use your mouth to taste, grab, pull and chew everything you can. This is known as 'mouthing' and does not indicate ill-intent.

As a puppy, your teeth are pin-sharp. Your owner will teach you not to bite or use heavy jaw pressure because these teeth can inadvertently hurt others, causing them to yelp and stop playing with you. Human skin is thin compared to dogs and does not have a layer of fur! Your owner's job is to teach you not to chew on their limbs or clothes by gently redirecting you onto tasty, appropriate toys that you can chew to your heart's content.

Puppies chew on flexible items such as shoes and laces because it helps soothe the pain of cutting adult teeth.

Misinterpreting your owner

Your owner will need patience to deal with your lively behaviour and needs to understand the need for slow, deliberate teaching. If a person shrieks, dodges away rapidly or pushes you roughly when you grab their trouser leg, this resembles the rough-and-tumble play that you enjoy in interactions with other puppies, so you're likely to misread it as 'Let's play!' rather than 'Don't do that!' This means that a loud, fast kind of reaction reinforces your coarse play style and means you are likely to be even rougher in future, not more gentle. It is wrong for owners to shout or squirt water at you, too, because this would teach you to fear humans and make it hard for you to integrate comfortably into human life.

Exploratory play

Many owners say that their dogs are attracted to shoes and like to chew them. They have also found that their dogs have a fondness for stealing socks and anything that is novel or has been recently moved by another family member (and smells of them). While inconvenient, this kind of exploration is one of the most important ways you teach yourself about the world. As you approach maturity and your curiosity wanes, such behaviours will naturally diminish, so a wise owner will simply prevent access to valuable property and clothing when you are young.

You may also ingest items that are either toxic or too large to pass readily through your gastrointestinal tract, causing a blockage. These may be chewed parts of your possessions, children's toys, or even stones. This

7 STEPS TO SLEEP

1 Ensure the puppy has toileted.

2 Provide a crate or safe den that has a comfortable bed and a worn item of owner's clothing to carry scent.

3 Add hollow chew toys into crate (these may contain your puppy's favourite food, such as liver paté).

4 Open the crate door so the puppy walks (or runs) in to reach the toys.

5 Allow 15-20 minutes of settling time. Stroke the puppy gently to help him to settle (no active games).

6 Drape a large sheet over two-thirds of the crate to block light while adjusting, then cover completely once asleep.

7 If the puppy cries, speak calmly and allow him to sniff your hand. Repeat this as necessary while the puppy settles.

happens quite commonly, but it can be life-threatening; you need to be examined by your vet at the earliest opportunity if your owner suspects you have eaten any items that may cause you harm.

Puppy sleeping at night

A puppy instinctively makes a noise to assist the mother in finding him when he is lost or separated. This is normal behaviour, but owners often complain that their puppy is 'crying' at night. Recommendations about this have changed. Rather than allowing the puppy to cope alone, owners are now advised to keep the puppy nearby while he adjusts to the new environment and loss of his previous litter and mother. Once the transition has begun, the puppy can be gradually moved to the family's preferred sleeping area. This allows everyone to adjust more readily.

Adolescence

Speed of development varies between breeds and genders, but adolescence occurs at around 4–12 months of age, with most dogs reaching sexual maturity at 10–12 months. During adolescence, your body grows continuously, helped by hormones that will affect your behaviour and how you appear to other dogs.

During adolescence, your motor capacities improve in terms of strength and skill, rather than any new ones emerging. Your body will continue to change, however. Your adult coat will start to show, usually manifesting at first as a strip along your spine which then spreads along either side of your body over the course of a few months. Your owner may miss seeing your puppy fluff as your limbs and muzzle grow longer too, giving you a gangly look. You will have your adult teeth, but may still like to chew and explore with your mouth.

Marking territory

Females experience their first oestrus cycle (known as 'being on heat' or 'in season') during adolescence, and males may show more interest in females at this time.

As you enter adolescence, your coat may look scruffy for a while as it changes from 'fluffy puppy' to adult.

Both males and females may also begin scent marking. Male dogs characteristically do this by lifting a leg to squirt a small amount of urine onto a vertical surface and they may do this repeatedly on walks. Females may squat over previous sites of urination from others. For all dogs, information is contained in scent, so this is another way you communicate your existence to others. Males may use it as a means to mark territory, while females may use it to advertise their whereabouts to potential mates.

Fear and fighting

You may squabble with other dogs more than previously during adolescence. Males may attempt to fight off potential competition, and females may too – the reasons for conflict between dogs can become complicated and often need expert unravelling to ascertain the causes. Research has shown that a 'second sensitive period' seems to occur during adolescence, and dogs may show heightened sensitivity to fear-arousing stimuli shortly before or after achieving sexual maturity. For this reason an unpleasant experience at this time can leave a previously calm dog feeling traumatized.

Neutering, where the male testicles (castration) or female ovaries (spaying) are removed by surgery, is known to influence various aspects of sexually dimorphic behaviour (reactions that are specific to male or female). These surgical operations may have health benefits and prevents unwanted litters, but may not resolve behavioural issues that owners report to be problematic (see pages 166–83).

THE OLDER PUPPY

As a puppy grows, he passes through many stages of development, in the same
way as a human child does when moving towards adulthood. The adolescent stage
requires extra patience, as the dog moves from puppyhood to adult.

Growing puppy

As the young puppy grows towards adolescence,
he begins to learn at an incredible rate. He is
curious, outgoing, eager to please and ready to
begin socialization, which must occur within the
time-sensitive period of 3-12 weeks. At eight
weeks he may experience a 'fear' period.

Adolescent (Juvenile)

From 12-17 weeks, puppies enter adolescence. They
grow rapidly, shed their puppy fur and lose their
baby teeth (chewing returns intensely for a time).
Limbs extend and hormonal changes bring about
sexual maturity. Fear periods may occur at two
points: 12 and 16/17 weeks.

Adult (1 year+)

Dogs become 'young adults' at 6-18 months.
They are still energetic and keen to learn, but
have more skills and learning in place than a
juvenile. This is a good time to increase the
scope of dog activities and the level of training
to maintain interest. Socialization continues to
be important. Young dogs, both male and female,
will include mating behaviours as part of their
play. This can be seen as a rehearsal for the
'real thing' and it may be directed at other dogs,
humans, and even inanimate objects such as
their dog beds or cushions.

6
EMOTION, CHARACTER AND NURTURE

Scientists have only recently begun to hypothesize that animals
have emotions, but many owners say that their dogs show the
same emotions as themselves. What is going on between your
pricked up ears when you hear your owner coming home?
Is it emotion that drives you to run to the door to meet them?

Emotion and awareness

The US psychobiologist Jaak Panksepp has identified seven primary process emotional systems, based on defined neural systems in the subcortical areas of the brain: Seeking, Rage, Fear, Lust, Care, Panic and Play. These 'ancestral tools for living' are part of the survival system, guiding animals towards safety.

The seven emotional systems identified by Jaak Panksepp stem from the most primitive responses in animals; he claims that emotions form the basis of (and so pre-exist) thoughts, and provide motivation for actions. Without a Seeking system, for instance, a puppy would not be motivated to reunite with the mother or have any interest in exploration. Without Fear, you would put yourself in unnecessary danger – this emotion drives the fight/flight system to move you out of danger. Without Play you could not experience happiness. Lust provides the necessary drive to procreate and Care leads you to nurture your young. Rage is the basis for anger, which serves to fuel the hormone systems for fighting. Panic registers separation distress and accounts for why a puppy might whimper in distress when left alone.

That's me!

When an adult human gazes at their reflection in a mirror, they are immediately aware that they are looking at themselves. Of course, what appears in the mirror is not truly 'there' – it is what the brain 'thinks' it sees given the reflected light. Recognizing a reflection as your own is an important indicator of 'self-awareness' – but does your canine brain recognize 'self' in a mirror? A dog that barks at its reflection may not realize that the image is his own. He may simply get used to the appearance of a

Human babies have been found to identify themselves in mirrors at 18 months of age. Prior to this they do not seem to recognize the image as 'self' but merely as an interesting 'other'.

similar 'dog-shape' as he wanders past and eventually stop looking at it. In scientific tests for self-awareness using mirrors, dogs have failed to recognize themselves.

Other dogs are different

How aware are you of yourself relative to other dogs? US evolutionary biologist Marc Bekoff suggests that your sense of smell gives you much more detailed information than you gain from your sight. He reasoned that perhaps a sense of 'self' and 'other' could be investigated using scent instead. Bekoff collected data from separate areas of snow on which his dog and that of others had urinated. This 'yellow snow' was collected and he timed how long his dog spent sniffing at it. The yellow snow that contained his own dog's scent was sniffed at by the dog for a much shorter time than that of other dogs. It seems that you do have a sense of your own scent compared to that of others.

You are able to make fine distinctions between smells, including being able to discriminate between your own and another dog's urine. Bekoff has suggested that perhaps your sense of self relies on a composite signal resulting from combining information from all your senses.

When tested, dogs were curious about 'the dog in the mirror' but showed no signs of recognizing it as 'self'.

A guide to your world

Your world today encompasses many things that your ancestors never experienced. This means that you will need to become habituated to them during the socialization phase in order not to become fearful of them. The most common things that dogs need to be exposed to from an early age are given here.

As a puppy, any sudden or unexpected event can startle you, but your world needs to slowly become as ordinary and predictable as possible. Meeting these situations during the socialization phase with your owner, who may pair them with enjoyable things, such as a treat or gentle petting, will give you confidence the next time they occur.

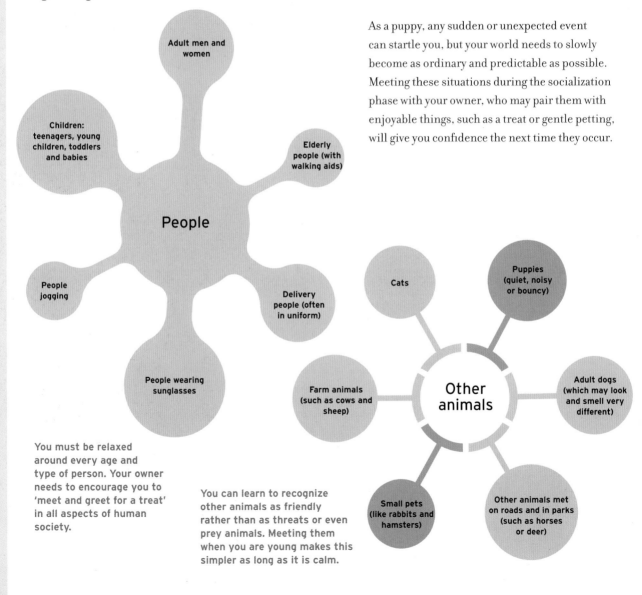

People

Adult men and women

Children: teenagers, young children, toddlers and babies

Elderly people (with walking aids)

People jogging

Delivery people (often in uniform)

People wearing sunglasses

Other animals

Cats

Puppies (quiet, noisy or bouncy)

Adult dogs (which may look and smell very different)

Farm animals (such as cows and sheep)

Small pets (like rabbits and hamsters)

Other animals met on roads and in parks (such as horses or deer)

You must be relaxed around every age and type of person. Your owner needs to encourage you to 'meet and greet for a treat' in all aspects of human society.

You can learn to recognize other animals as friendly rather than as threats or even prey animals. Meeting them when you are young makes this simpler as long as it is calm.

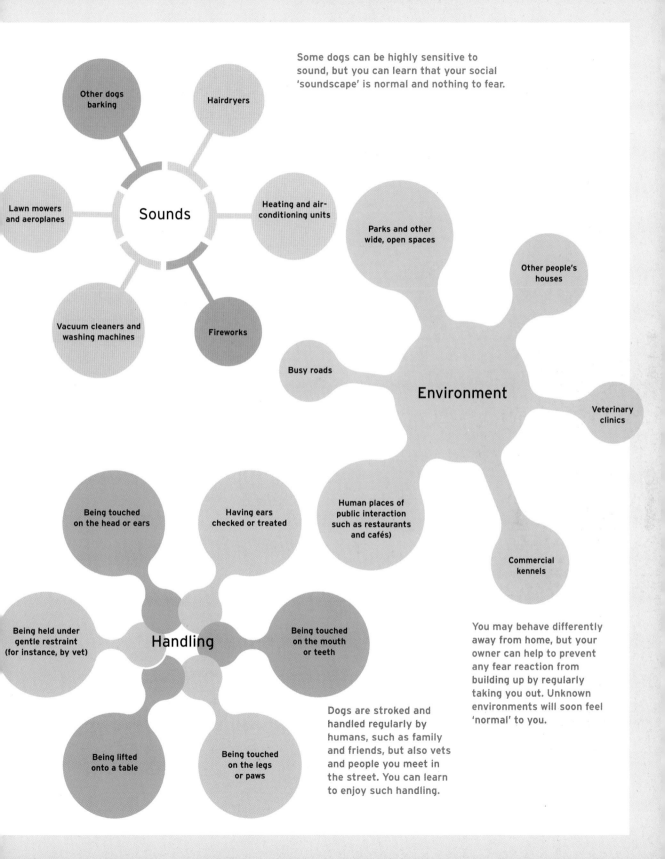

Some dogs can be highly sensitive to sound, but you can learn that your social 'soundscape' is normal and nothing to fear.

Other dogs barking

Hairdryers

Lawn mowers and aeroplanes

Sounds

Heating and air-conditioning units

Vacuum cleaners and washing machines

Fireworks

Parks and other wide, open spaces

Other people's houses

Busy roads

Environment

Veterinary clinics

Human places of public interaction such as restaurants and cafés)

Commercial kennels

Being touched on the head or ears

Having ears checked or treated

Being held under gentle restraint (for instance, by vet)

Handling

Being touched on the mouth or teeth

Being lifted onto a table

Being touched on the legs or paws

You may behave differently away from home, but your owner can help to prevent any fear reaction from building up by regularly taking you out. Unknown environments will soon feel 'normal' to you.

Dogs are stroked and handled regularly by humans, such as family and friends, but also vets and people you meet in the street. You can learn to enjoy such handling.

Human vs dog emotions

As science has shown, humans and other animals, such as dogs, have seven basic emotions that relate to subcortical brain processes. But people commonly refer to dogs as feeling considerably more emotions, such as jealousy, anger, love and happiness. Is this the case?

In the past, the idea that dogs feel emotions, just like humans, has been interpreted as anthropomorphism or 'personification', intimating that as a dog you cannot feel the same way as a human might in response to a situation. This is difficult to prove, because in order for humans to know what you feel, you would need to describe it in words. However, during the 20th century, behavioural scientists such as B.F. Skinner insisted that observations could be made about your basic emotional states without the need to delve much further, as what you do illustrates much about your current emotional state.

Degrees of emotion

It is normal to describe 'alarm' in any species, but the identification of states like 'anger' or 'fear' in mammals has largely been based on pattern-recognition – that is to say, by examining what behaviour is observed at a particular point. For instance, fleeing or freezing when confronted with a threat is taken as a demonstration of fear. But how much emotional subtlety are you able to feel and show, and how well are we humans able to understand you? Neuroimaging studies have indicated that people can accurately assess a dog's subjective state by the tone of their bark, and dogs can assess ours, too. It seems both sides of this partnership are hardwired to recognize and react to 'happy sounds' via the auditory cortex in the brain and can register subtle changes.

Humans willingly state that their pets love them, show happiness when they are together and miss them when they are absent. These beliefs are fundamental to your presence in your owner's life as a pet; if there was no such emotional relationship, you might not be a pet at all. This bond seems to be real – most cats run away when scared, but many dogs run to their owners.

Understanding each other

Research on compatibility indicates that dog owners experience improved mental health and greater wellbeing when they feel their pet's behaviour is compatible with their own. In situations where the relationship has broken down (with dogs exhibiting problem behaviours), owners may report that they no longer wish to keep their dog. Behaviour counselling can reframe emotional description in a way that correctly reflects the dog's emotions, replacing those the owner has wrongly assumed. It seems that communication is good between the species, but not always reliable.

Sometimes a human and dog perfectly match in emotion, such as when both have been happily playing in the park.

HAVING FUN OR UNDER STRESS?

Here, the person stroking the dog is enjoying the contact, but the dog is showing retreat signals and does not want to be touched. We can see the retreat signals in the dog's behaviour: he is trying to lean away from the human; his ears are back and his head is turned away; his eyes are looking at the person stroking, perhaps assessing the possible threat. The dog is also licking his lips, a sign of conflicted feelings.

A baby may be allowed to crawl all over a dog. Parents may even consider this to be cute and friendly. However, this dog is showing protective behaviour over his toy: he has become very still, with a tense body. In this situation his head may turn away, and he may or may not growl but his eyes will glare. Any chewing will slow down and the tail will stop wagging. These are subtle, often silent, but important warnings.

When a puppy playfully 'mouths' a person, this may be mistaken by a person as an attack, when in fact he is just playing as he would with another puppy. He may grab a trouser leg because it is flapping around; if the human tugs it in return (to get away), the puppy may see it as a game. He may pant, with the corners of his mouth drawn back in a loose manner, and tail wagging. The unmistakeable 'play bow' sees the dog's bottom in the air and his front end crouching low.

When a dog begins pulling on his lead, he may simply be trying to sniff something. The owner may pull back, worrying that the dog is pulling her over. She may mistakenly think that the dog is stubborn and angry with her. Often humans exacerbate this situation by holding the lead up high or pulling it tight. This means the dog cannot move, so leans away further, in an effort to continue sniffing.

Humans may think that two dogs are fighting when they are simply playing. The dogs' body language gives the most accurate information. A 'play bow' (where the dogs' front end is lowered and the rear end is in the air, tail wagging) is a sign of enjoyment and a wish to continue. Dogs also 'jaw wrestle', gripping one anothers' mouths loosely and gently.

Emotional body language

It seems that you do have emotions and try to show them to us humans, but we don't always understand correctly. For instance, 'wagging your tail' is popularly interpreted as a signal that you are friendly, but this is not entirely correct. You may wag your tail when aroused, agitated or upset.

Adults often tell children that if a dog is wagging its tail, it is friendly and happy. However, while this is sometimes true, we have to look at the tail carriage for full and accurate information. If you are holding your tail at mid-height, you are probably relaxed. If you are holding your tail in an upward direction, you are alert – and the higher it raises, the more agitated you are. An upright tail means 'Back off!' On the other hand, a tucked-under tail indicates that you are trying to appease or feeling ill.

The intensity of the tail wag and its speed also communicate your emotional state (a slight, slow wag

is a cautious 'hello', while a broad wag is friendly. Tiny, high-speed movements signify that you are just about to do something, like run or fight. Tail behaviour as emotional signifier can cause problems, as some breeds have tails that are naturally curled high above their back. Docking of tails (where the tail is artificially shortened) can also adversely affect this exceptional communicator, which can complicate your relationship with other dogs.

Guilty look

When your owner has been away and returns to find you have chewed the chair leg or toileted on the floor, he or she may tell other humans that you 'knew' that you had done wrong because of the guilty look on your face. Can you really feel this kind of remorse for an act, and can you understand that something you did a while before your owner admonished you has had an adverse impact on your owner and family?

For you to feel 'guilt' you would need to be aware *while doing something* that at some point in the future, this act would make your caregiver unhappy. Since this would require a high degree of self-awareness and also the ability to link current events to future or past ones, it is unlikely that you are able to feel bad or in any way 'guilty' about your actions.

Instead it is likely that as an expert reader of human emotion, you are aware that your owner is angry when

Humans can read your emotions via your body language, but their interpretation may not be accurate.

COMMUNICATING BY TAIL

Wagging to the right

Wagging to the left

Dogs have been found to wag their tails more to the right when presented with their owner or someone they would like to approach. When dogs observe other dogs with right-wagging tails, they show signs of increased relaxation.

Dogs wag their tails more to the left when faced with someone or thing they would like to retreat from, such as an unfamiliar dog with an aggressive stance. Dogs observing others whose tails were wagging to the left showed signs of increased anxiety.

they raise their voice and perhaps shake a pointing hand. You will then show body signals in response to their actions, which relate not to your earlier (forgotten) action, but their current state, which may arouse feelings of fear, discomfort or anticipation of punishment in you. You may lower your head, look up at your owner, fold your ears back and even roll on your back. These are known as appeasement signals, and they are designed to avoid the dangerous ire of humans from becoming worse. Skilled as you are in linking events together, you will have linked your owner behaving in this way with punishment, even though you have no way of telling what they are upset about, and your owner may mistakenly say that you 'know' what the problem is and 'feel guilty'.

How do you feel?

Your emotional state not only affects how you feel, but also affects the judgements you make about the friendliness or hostile nature of other animals, humans and situations. At times your emotions may deliver up accurate information, but at others they may be confused by the past.

In 2010, British Professor of Animal Welfare Michael Mendl and his team found that dogs clearly demonstrated 'optimistic' or 'pessimistic' outlooks, which affected their judgements and expectations. In experiments, dogs were taught that dog bowls full of food could be found at one end of a room, while empty bowls sat at the other end. The researchers then placed food bowls around the centre of the room to see what would happen. Dogs that had shown little anxiety on separation from their owners ran up to the bowls (seemingly optimistic of finding them full), while more anxious dogs were slow to approach them (seemingly expecting them to be empty).

Depression and jealousy

It is thought that dogs may also experience long-term negative emotions akin to human depression. In 1965, US psychologist Martin Seligman examined how long a dog would work to avoid something unpleasant (in this

In studies, dogs that see another dog being rewarded for a task that they completed without reward have stopped performing the task and shown signs of frustration.

case, electric shocks were given to the dogs, which would no longer be allowed on ethical grounds). Eventually, the dogs stopped trying to escape the electric shocks, and were said to be in a condition known as 'learned helplessness'. They showed long-term symptoms of the stress following the experiment similar to those seen in humans suffering from clinical depression.

Your owner may say you become 'jealous' when other dogs are around, especially if you feel that your owner is likely to give them a treat that you might enjoy. This idea was tested by US psychologist Christine Harris in 2014, whose team found that dogs exhibit significantly more competitive behaviours – such as getting between an owner and object, or pushing against one of them – when their owners displayed affectionate behaviour towards another dog. The scientists hypothesized that jealousy may have a primordial form, designed to protect social bonds from interlopers.

In 2008, Dr Friederike Range of the University of Vienna showed that dogs performing a simple task will stop performing that task when another dog is rewarded for a parallel task. Dogs were trained to offer a paw to gain a food reward. Then one dog continued to be given food while the other did not. As expected, the dog not given the food slowed and then stopped offering the paw. However, it also showed signs of frustration that the other dog continued to be rewarded for the task.

HOW YOU FEEL ABOUT...

...YOUR TERRITORY

Territorial instinct is a natural feature, necessary for your survival, and you value your surroundings and home very highly. This includes any garden area, either behind or in front of your home. Your territory may extend to places that you visit on regular walks.

As soon as you think these locations may be invaded by a competing dog you start to behave defensively, showing tension in your body posture. Your aim is to protect this area from another dog entering. This is particularly noticeable when it concerns your bed or favourite sofa at home.

In order to lower feelings of tension, other dogs can be given their own space away from yours. A staircase may help keep the peace. Your owner must teach all dogs in the home to calmly obey instructions so that ultimately the owner can defuse any possible territorial disagreements.

...YOUR POSSESSIONS

As a dog, your natural instinct is to survive. You value items that may be of use to you, including food but also other items like toys that your owner has provided or that you have chosen for yourself (such as a favourite old shoe or stick you like chewing). You are not designed to share possessions.

In the company of other dogs you may feel under threat when they show interest in these items. You defend by snatching and running away, or holding still and growling threateningly at the other dog. If the other dog takes the item, you will defend more vigorously in future and this can lead to serious injuries from fighting.

You can learn to relax around such items with careful training from your owner. You may even treat your human owner as a valuable possession, and try to prevent other dogs from getting near. If so, careful, expert training is necessary to help you learn that you are not under threat.

...SEXUAL CONFLICT

Hormonal influences can cause you to feel tense and defensive. Maturing male dogs may feel competitive amongst each other, and female dogs can become defensive around the time of their season. Sexual conflict issues usually occur between two dogs of the same sex, two littermates or between dogs of similar strength or temperament.

Neutering can remove this competitive drive, and can resolve situations based around hormonal fluctuations. However, once you have learned that something or someone may represent a threat, the memory may stay with you and continue to affect your behaviour in future. Neutering may not be a solution in situations of this type and will certainly not help if you are a male dog lacking in confidence, because the loss of testosterone resulting from castration may reduce your confidence still further, and lead to exacerbating the problem.

Analysing behaviour

Your behaviour is fascinating to humans, who endlessly wonder why you do what you do. Owners frequently report problems relating to their pet's behaviour which mystify them. You cannot tell humans what you are thinking, but through your actions they can realize what you like and dislike.

Misinterpretation of your reactions occasionally leads owners to employ harsh tactics when attempting to teach you new ways. This may be due to an erroneous assumption that a dog who is showing aggressive behaviour is displaying a natural need to become head of a supposed hierarchy or 'pack leader'. However, behaviour studies have shown that such reactions are more likely to relate to fear or protecting resources. Fortunately, behavioural science has taken a leap forward from outdated thoughts of constructs such as 'dominance' in dogs and now views things quite differently.

A-B-C analysis

The analysis of behaviour in animals is augmented by the human field, where ethical interventions have proved successful with adults and children, particularly in the teaching profession. Dr Susan Friedman, a psychology professor at Utah State University, USA, pioneered the application of Applied Behavior Analysis (ABA) to both companion and captive animals. This perspective focuses on a simple problem-solving model: either 'too much of the wrong behaviour' or 'not enough of the right behaviour', and may seek to influence either or both.

Behaviour in the ABA system is analysed in three parts: the 'Antecedent', which is the situation or environment preceding and influencing the production of behaviour; the 'Behaviour' itself (what is being observed and how frequently); and finally, the 'Consequence' which is the direct result of the behaviour. These form the unit A-B-C. This type of analysis allows behaviourists and caregivers to gather factual information to predict what an animal like you will do in future based on the reciprocal influence of the environment. It also enables them to plan interventions to adjust problem behaviours and teach new skills.

The approach to arranging consequences to increase or decrease behaviour is known as 'operant conditioning' or 'operant learning' and it traces back to the work of B.F. Skinner (see pages 68–69).

The A-B-C method supplies owners with clear guidance on how to steer dogs away from problem behaviour.

USING THE A-B-C METHOD

Unpleasant experience

A

The owner ignores any avoidance signals from the dog and attempts to clip his claws. The dog is forced to keep still.

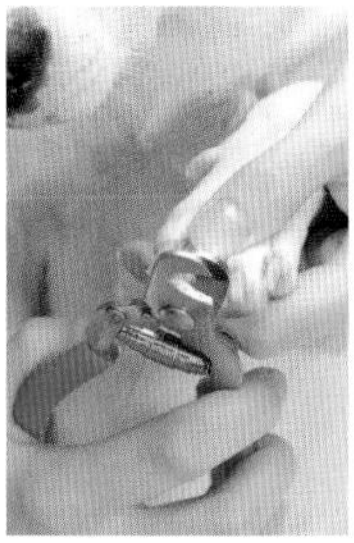

B

The dog responds by biting the clippers or the owner; this is a sign that the dog is very uncomfortable.

C

As a result, the owner stops attempting to clip the claws. The bite was successful in achieving this. The dog will probably bite when clipped again in future.

Pleasant experience

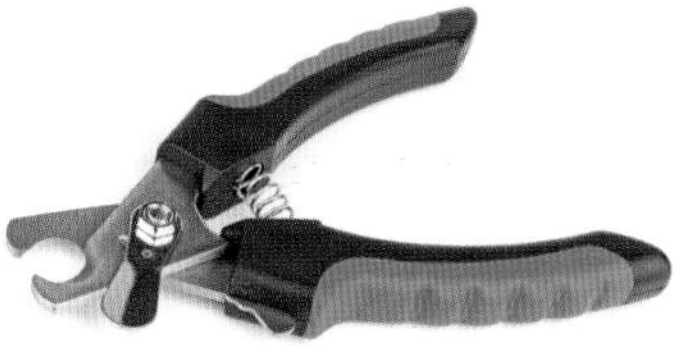

A

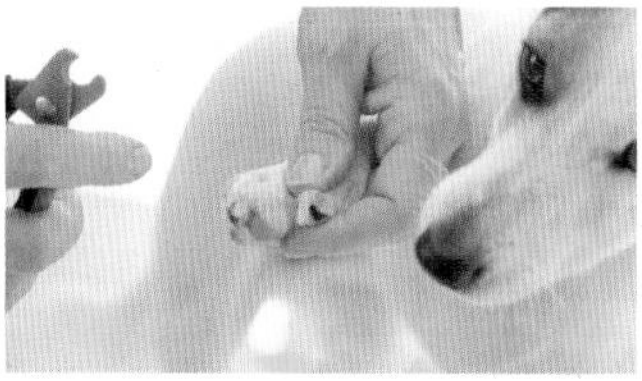

B

The owner approaches the dog with the clipper but at any time the dog wishes to move away, he is allowed to do so.

C

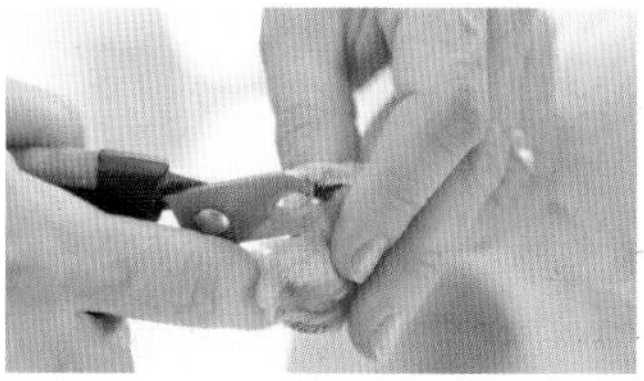

The dog is allowed to choose to offer his paw. This can be trained separately at first using tasty food to lure the dog.

As a result of the calm behaviour, the dog earns a valuable reward in the form of tasty food. The dog will allow more claw clipping in future.

Gender differences

Does your owner describe your behaviour as 'typical' for a male or female? In this section we look at whether there are any sexually dimorphic behaviours (those due to sex differences) and the degree to which they are particular to one gender. Neutering blurs the lines still further.

Your owner might be surprised to see a female dog humping another dog or cushion, or cocking her leg to deposit small amounts of urine. In fact, this is part of the normal female social repertoire, even though such behaviours are popularly considered to be 'male'.

Owners may confuse gender with breed traits or looks; the female Staffordshire (top) may appear more 'masculine' to some than the male Papillon (bottom).

Effects of testosterone

In the uterus, puppy foetuses are exposed to greater or lesser amounts of testosterone, a hormone that promotes the development of male characteristics. Research suggests that if a female is positioned between two males in utero, her brain may experience masculinization, as testosterone diffuses through the amniotic membrane and through uterine blood flow. The bodily orientation of males to females while in the uterus is also thought to have an impact. This can lead to exaggerated 'male' behaviours such as frequent urine marking and confident displays of aggression.

Testosterone has also been found to affect the male dog's brain development in utero and in later puppy stages as the dog matures. It is thought that testosterone levels start to rise at around four to five months of age, peaking at 10 months. They then reduce to settle at around 18 months of age.

Spaying and neutering

Neutering is reported to have wide-ranging health benefits for both male and female dogs. In females, this includes reduction of mammary tumours and incidences of pyometra (womb infection). In males, it can reduce the chance of some cancers and the risk of prostate disease. Neither neutering nor spaying are guaranteed to eliminate aggressive behaviour.

Spaying (via an ovariohysterectomy) removes the ovaries and uterus in the female dog. These represent the sources of estrogen and progesterone, which fluctuate in cycles. Dog behaviours during these cycles can change dramatically, including nest building and an increase in protective actions, particularly over possessions. Pseudo- or phantom-pregnancy symptoms occasionally occur, where the female dog may produce milk and select objects to nurture, carrying out the kind of behaviours she would show towards a puppy.

Neutering the male dog (through gonadectomy) effectively removes the source of circulating testosterone, as the testicles are removed by castration. Given that the brain of a dog experiences the impact of testosterone even before birth, it is not surprising that 'male' behaviours continue even after neutering. It is possible for neutered males to cock their legs to urinate, continue sexually-oriented behaviours such as humping, and also to mate with a female fully (the main difference being that no puppies arise as a result).

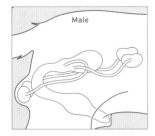

Male reproductive organs before neutering (testicles still in place).

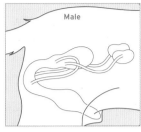

Male reproductive organs after neutering (testicles removed).

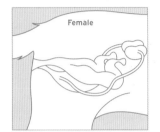

Female reproductive organs before spaying (uterus still in place).

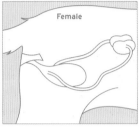

Female reproductive organs after spaying (uterus removed).

EFFECTS OF NEUTERING AND SPAYING

NEUTERING (males)	SPAYING (females)	HUMAN ADVANTAGES
Neutered dogs are less likely to roam, so less likely to go missing, get run over, or fight with other dogs. Unneutered dogs are likely to respond to a female dog in season up to a mile (1.6 km) away; they may become frustrated, bark and try to escape. Neutering results in a reduced incidence of prostate disease and a reduced risk of some cancers. An unneutered dog is more likely to be the target of attack from another dog. He is also more likely to show aggression to other dogs both on and off their leads.	Spaying reduces the risk of mammary cancer. There is also a lower likelihood of pyometra (womb infection). Eliminates the risk of pregnancy and giving birth. No false pregnancies occur after season (these can cause medical and behavioural problems). 	An unneutered dog is much more likely to 'hump'. If a female dog is in season she will attract male dogs. They may jump fences or break doors to get to the female, and bark loudly. Pregnancy, birth and looking after a litter is expensive; there may be 12 in one litter and they will need feeding before homing. Female dogs in season can produce discharge (bloody) for around three weeks. Each year thousands of unwanted dogs are put to sleep due to lack of suitable homes.

Keeping yourself fit

You need exercise, but research shows that 2.7 million dogs in the UK are exercised only in the home and garden. A 2008 study in Australia found that 23 per cent of dog owners never walk their dog, while in the USA, 'dog parks' are common, but the average daily dog walk lasts only 17 minutes.

Documented health benefits show that owning a dog increases physical activity and wellbeing through walking you and socializing, so ways are being researched to encourage humans to walk their dogs more. Guidelines for exercise suggest around two walks a day that amount to a total of one hour, on and off the lead. A vet can advise on whether or not you are receiving the right amount for your age and ability; you may only be able to walk a certain distance (if you are a puppy or older dog, for instance) and the vet will need to take this into account.

Studies indicate that by walking you daily for around half an hour, your owner will reach the minimum recommended exercise level of 150 minutes per week. Resolving behavioural issues such as pulling on the lead may encourage your owner to go for more walks. Projects are also underway to provide more appropriate 'dog-friendly' areas for walking.

How much is too much?

Owners often complain about their dog's excitable or very reactive behaviour during walks. If this is the case, it may be that you are still young and in need of additional exercise, or come from active working stock. On the other hand, you may only be responding to changes in the environment with heightened sensitivity to movement or noise. Dogs that are stressed for more general reasons are also likely to show signs of increased agitation.

In the natural world, dogs are most active around dawn and dusk, resting at other times. This is known as 'crepuscular activity'. The human timetable does not

The 'right' amount of exercise varies from dog to dog, but most dogs do not get enough physical activity.

always correspond with this natural set of needs and this can lead owners to complain that dogs are hyperactive at times when they themselves would like to rest.

Struggling to be calm

You may be hyperactive due to stress or overstimulation, and if so, may need more frequent rest in a peaceful place. You certainly don't need punishment for racing or jumping around, as this will cause a nervous, defensive reaction. Characteristically, your activity level should reduce as you age. If an older dog is not able to settle in quiet conditions, a veterinary check may be advised to determine whether there is a neurological disturbance related to pain or illness. True hyperkinesis (hyperactivity) may be a sign of abnormalities in the dopaminergic, serotonergic or noradrenergic systems, but there is little scientific evidence for this at present.

DOES YOUR OWNER WALK YOU ENOUGH?

Walks off the lead

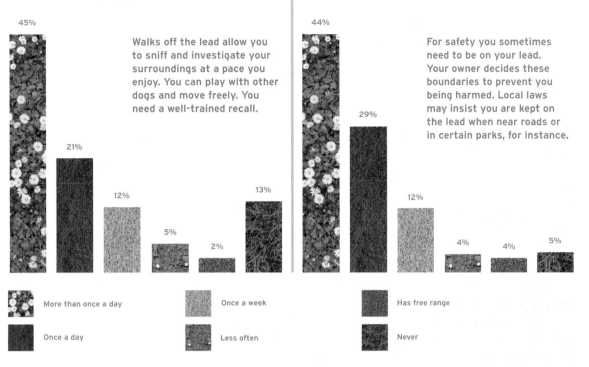

Walks off the lead allow you to sniff and investigate your surroundings at a pace you enjoy. You can play with other dogs and move freely. You need a well-trained recall.

45%
21%
12%
5%
2%
13%

Walks on the lead

For safety you sometimes need to be on your lead. Your owner decides these boundaries to prevent you being harmed. Local laws may insist you are kept on the lead when near roads or in certain parks, for instance.

44%
29%
12%
4%
4%
5%

- More than once a day
- Once a day
- Once a week
- Less often
- Has free range
- Never

How long is your walk for?

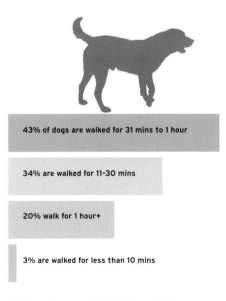

43% of dogs are walked for 31 mins to 1 hour

34% are walked for 11-30 mins

20% walk for 1 hour+

3% are walked for less than 10 mins

Exercise is a matter of quality as well as quantity, and it is also good for your owner's health!

All figures taken from PDSA PAW Report 2015

Keeping yourself busy

Living as a companion to a human being is rewarding but challenging too. You will have to get used to a huge range of activities and be prepared to spend time without any company. It is important that you have activities during this time to keep you physically and mentally fit.

Some of the best ideas for keeping animals active in confinement have come from the care of captive animals. Environmental enrichment is one such idea. This has evolved from the understanding that it is not possible to provide all the complexities of a natural, wild environment, but there are ways of enriching a man-made, limited environment.

Physical enrichment is gained by adding interesting structures to an environment so an animal has things to interact with. Cognitive enrichment can be provided through the provision of problem-solving activities. This may be combined with nutritional enrichment, so that different types and textures of food are offered in unlikely, random and scattered places (rather than in one routine place), and possibly in puzzle boxes. Sensory enrichment can also be offered through the thoughtful use of sound, light and smell.

Calming sound

Kennel environments can be noisy (exceeding 100 dB, or the equivalent of a busy factory) and may exacerbate stress. Bioacoustic research, which looks at how sounds influence living organisms, suggests that classical music can be used to calm dogs in these environments, helping to reduce the level of barking and even encourage dogs to spend more time sitting and lying down. In one study, male dogs responded better than females. In another piece of innovative research, the type of music played was seen to have an impact: heavy-metal music was the least beneficial in effect and actually increased barking.

As a guide, tempos matching heart rates are calming for you and your fellow dogs. Pure tones and regular rhythms are also associated with positive effect. But grinding or harsh tones with negative states (think of growling or loud rebukes) increase feelings of stress.

Dogs are highly sensitive to the differing patterns of soundwaves, such as classical music (bottom) and electronic music (top).

Water therapy

If you are suffering from reduced mobility or joint disorders, or recovering from surgery, one of the best forms of exercise is hydrotherapy, where you can gently exercise in warm water. Cold water can reduce blood flow to extremities and may put undue pressure on your heart as you exercise, but warm water is therapeutic. Your muscles work against the resistance of the water without pressure being placed on joints. Hydrotherapy allows you to exercise without the dangers associated with open water such as the risk of becoming entangled in submerged objects or infection from toxic bacteria such as Cyanobacteria (also known as blue-green algae) found in freshwater areas.

Hydrotherapy is a safe and effective way for dogs to exercise when their mobility is reduced for any reason.

Mental activities

Interactive toys such as hollow toys with food inside that you must chew to retrieve; foraging games such as food or toys hidden inside a box or under a blanket; puzzle toys with levers and spinners that you must learn to open and manipulate to reach the goodies inside; balls containing food that you must roll around to get food to drop out. Timed feeders that beep when food is released will also encourage you to seek the feeder throughout the day.

Physical activities

Gentle and low-impact physical activities such as swimming, hydrotherapy or going for a rambling walk with plenty of smells.

Medium-impact activities such as playing in hosepipe water/spray fountains, walking with another dog, obedience training, rally competition, searching for hidden toys, playing hide and seek with your owner.

High-impact activities such as flyball, treiball, chasing thrown toys or disks, cross country running, hiking.

Going to school

While it is popularly assumed that you and other dogs require training, this may not be performed in a formal situation. Many owners train their dogs in the commands for 'Sit', 'Stay', 'Come' and 'Fetch' but there is much more that can be taught, and socialization skills may be the most important of all.

In 2015, The Peoples Dispensary for Sick Animals (PDSA), based in the UK, reported that according to owners, 60 per cent of dogs (around 5.5 million) did not attend training classes in their first six months. This is a 10 per cent decrease on the previous year, indicating that fewer dogs are attending training school. In the USA, figures for formal training of dogs in 1999 showed that only around 25 per cent of owners participated in formal training classes.

Unnecessary euthanasia

Alongside this data, two-thirds of veterinary professionals in the UK reported an increase of attacks between dogs. Almost the same number reported an increase in dog euthanasia as a result of behavioural issues. In the USA, over a million dogs are euthanized each year, according to the American Humane Society, and many of these are taken to shelters by their owners because of problem behaviours – such as biting, aggression and destructiveness – that could have been improved with formal training. A 2001 report on the problem by Philip Kass *et al.* found that the following breeds were most likely to be euthanized at their owner's request because of behavioural problems: German Shepherds, Cocker Spaniels, Staffordshire Terriers, Labrador Retrievers, Chihuahuas, Chow Chows, and Rottweilers.

Learning to live with people

Going to a small dog training class run by a registered, qualified instructor will teach you to get along with other dogs and people. Where positive, reward-based training methods are used, you will learn patterns of interaction with humans that are always beneficial. Dogs trained with such methods have been shown to display fewer problem behaviours compared to those taught using punishment-based techniques.

Dogs that are trained and engage in shared activities with their owners are interpreted by others to be friendlier, scoring lower in problem behaviours such as disobedience, aggression, nervousness, anxiety, destructiveness and excitability.

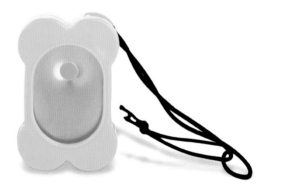

A 'clicker' is used in training to make a clear sound which the dog associates with a correct choice. Whistles can be used in place of verbal cues.

FLYBALL RELAY COURSE

Energetic dogs benefit from being trained to perform in dog sports, and the fast pace of a sport such as flyball combines enthusiasm with control. Flyball is a fast-paced, energetic dog sport where two teams of four dogs compete. The dogs run a short course over hurdles towards a box containing a ball, which each dog retrieves in turn. The fastest team wins the race.

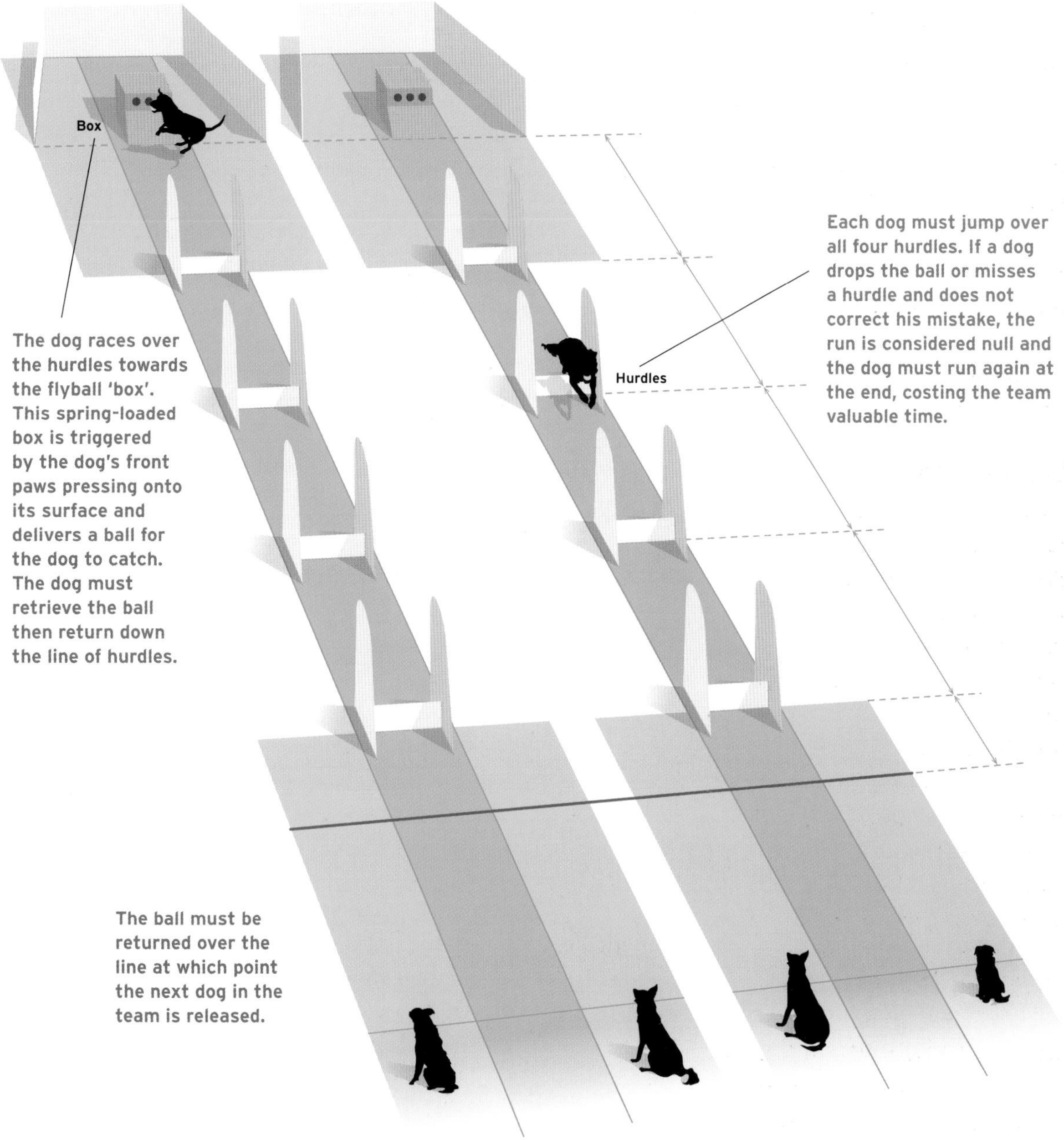

Box

Each dog must jump over all four hurdles. If a dog drops the ball or misses a hurdle and does not correct his mistake, the run is considered null and the dog must run again at the end, costing the team valuable time.

Hurdles

The dog races over the hurdles towards the flyball 'box'. This spring-loaded box is triggered by the dog's front paws pressing onto its surface and delivers a ball for the dog to catch. The dog must retrieve the ball then return down the line of hurdles.

The ball must be returned over the line at which point the next dog in the team is released.

Linking it all together

It is your owner's responsibility to teach you to connect useful activities together rather than inappropriate or unwanted ones. There are many different training methods but invasive methods such as punishment or compulsion (moulding) may have negative physical or emotional side effects.

Some things that dogs can be trained to do make the most of their natural behaviours, which can easily be adapted for new uses. For instance, when you are trained to walk calmly next to your owner, sit or lie down next to them, or perhaps pick up the post and bring it safely back, it is easy to see how these are new forms of action based on natural dog behaviours.

You will not respond well to compulsive training methods that rely on punishment, such as moulding. This is a method of pushing or manipulating the dog into position. You may not enjoy being pushed into a sit, as it risks injury to your spine and hips, and is painful. Your owner needs to learn less-invasive methods such

as lure-reward, shaping and chaining, which have been shown to have more positive, motivational impact.

Luring and reward

This is one of the easiest ways for your owner to teach you how to 'sit'. It involves your owner placing a piece of food on your nose, so that you sniff it. As you do so, your owner begins to move the food upwards so that your head follows. By luring your head up, your bottom naturally drops down into a sitting position. As you reach the 'sit' position, your owner marks the behaviour by praising or using a clicker, then gives you the food.

Shaping something new

Training you means reinforcing (or rewarding) successive approximations of the target behaviour until you have reached the level of training and behaviour that your owner wants. This process is referred to as 'shaping'. It is rather like moulding a pot from clay, where the final form is gradually created from the rough lumpy object into a polished, smooth and recognizable shape.

'Free-shaping' is a form of training where you are less directed by your tutor — they simply wait for you to do something they would like you to continue, then give you a reinforcer to encourage you to repeat it. Once your owner has the final result they would like; they add a 'cue' such as a word or hand signal to name the action so that you form a link. This way, they can ask you to perform it again in future. By producing the cue word at any time, you will respond with the desired behaviour.

Dogs naturally watch human movements, so prompting, with a food lure in the hand, is an effective way to teach a hand cue.

LURING

1 The 'clicker' provides a clear marker, or signal, that the dog is about to get a good reward.

2 The lure, usually food, must be strongly scented enough to cause the dog to pay attention. The hand containing the lure is what the dog's head follows.

4 As the luring hand lifts, so does the dog's head. The dog's nose is following the target hand and can be lured into a wide variety of positions.

3 As the hand containing the lure drops lower, so the dog's head lowers to follow it. To encourage a dog to lie down, its head must follow the lure in a downward motion.

Chaining forward and back

Once individual behaviours have been shaped, they can be linked together in a chain. This means that you can perform sophisticated tasks when cued. Some of the actions in the chain are taught in reverse order. This is so that you know the final result first, and puts what you are learning into context. A dog taught to drop a ball through a hoop is taught by forward and backward chaining. The dog is taught to: hold a ball (forward chaining); place the ball in the hoop; walk to the hoop with the ball; pick up and carry the ball to the hoop; and drop it through (backward chaining). The dog then collects the ball to complete the cycle.

You can be trained to link together a series of actions, such as scoring 'goals' on a mini basketball hoop or posting a letter through a letterbox.

7
YOU AND OTHER DOGS

If you share your home with one or more dogs, you may get along well or occasionally fight. The fact that you are conspecifics (members of the same species) does not automatically lead to mutual acceptance and accord. This chapter looks at the complexities of inter-canine relationships.

Who is in charge?

In the past, dogs were thought to have a 'pack' mentality, like wolves, that led them to recognize dominant others (dogs or humans). However, wolves only resort to hierarchical behaviours when they are confined or short of resources, and in any case, dogs and wolves are only distantly related.

As a companion animal, it is in your interest to behave in a way that promotes your key relationship (with your owner) and ensures an ongoing, beneficial situation. It serves you better to establish amicable relationships with the humans, dogs and other pets in your family than be aggressive towards them, as this might ultimately threaten your survival (through loss of a safe home).

You and your owner have an amicable relationship that rests on mutual respect and companionship.

You can be seen to form paired relationships with your species and others, and this will be demonstrated in behaviours such as turn-taking and even self-handicapping (playing at the other person's or dog's level) to allow play to continue. You may find that you and your dog friends value resources differently; a harmonious relationship could be easily built if you enjoy food and value it highly, while your companion dog values social contact with humans more highly (see opposite page). In this way the competitive drive is reduced and with it, the potential for conflict.

You will happily 'follow' a benevolent, predictable and rewarding 'leader' (usually your owner) without any need for them to use force. Your owner already has control over time and resources – such as when you go out for walks, or what you eat and when. A healthy owner–dog relationship is more like that of carer and family member, or teacher and student, than despot and cowering servant.

Punishing tactics

Sadly, in the past, and in the name of 'dominant' behaviour, dogs have been harshly punished for what is incorrectly described as over-confidence when in fact, they are manifesting self-protection through fear of harm, or resource protection (see pages 114–115). Harsh 'dominance reduction' methods often increase the intensity of aggressive outbursts, putting both the dog and others around them at risk. Fortunately, animal welfare laws have begun to address such approaches.

SHARING RESOURCES

Potential conflict between dogs often centres around resources. However, by identifying each dog's priorities it is possible to encourage and increase harmony.

Differing values

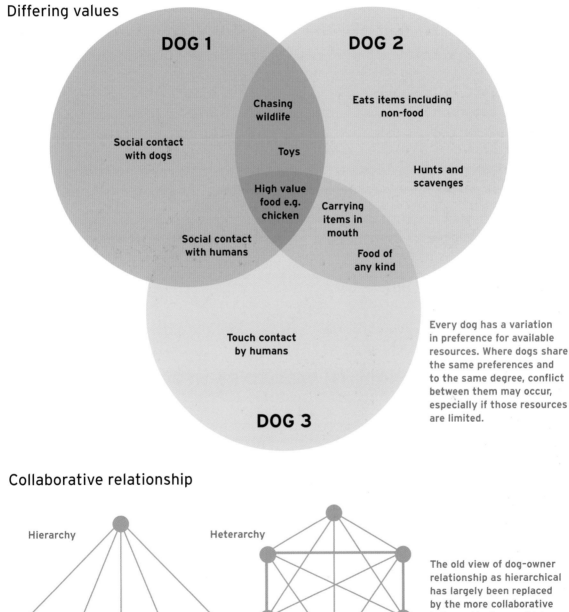

DOG 1

DOG 2

Chasing wildlife

Toys

Social contact with dogs

Eats items including non-food

Hunts and scavenges

High value food e.g. chicken

Carrying items in mouth

Social contact with humans

Food of any kind

Touch contact by humans

DOG 3

Every dog has a variation in preference for available resources. Where dogs share the same preferences and to the same degree, conflict between them may occur, especially if those resources are limited.

Collaborative relationship

Hierarchy

Heterarchy

The old view of dog-owner relationship as hierarchical has largely been replaced by the more collaborative heterarchical one, which values dog and owner needs.

What motivates you?

Your daily life will consist of a mixture of things that you enjoy and that help you feel secure, along with a few situations that you tolerate but may rather avoid. Importantly, this range of likes and dislikes varies for each dog, and by knowing your preferences your owner will find it easier to motivate you.

Every healthy animal seeks to maintain a sense of wellbeing or state of 'emotional homeostasis'. If this balance is compromised in some way, you will attempt to rebalance it by acting in certain ways – so how you feel drives your behaviour. You may want to play, and so fetch a toy and drop it in your owner's lap. You might feel an urge to reproduce, but in the absence of a willing female your owner may notice you humping your bed or a visitor's leg. That you experience these motivations is not in question; because the feelings that drive them stem from the areas of the primal brain (see pages 104–105).

Dealing with conflict

For your owner, the most important thing is to notice the way that you choose to act in respect of these motivations. In the park, would you rather stay with your owner, or run off and play with other dogs? Do you feel very motivated to defend your space on the sofa, or do you willingly move away when challenged?

The theory of 'Resource Holding Potential' (RHP) suggested by British biologist Geoff Parker (1974) looks at a dog's relative level of perseverance should a conflict arise over something of value. Are you the dog

TRAINING WITH VALUED REINFORCERS

Relaxed behaviour, well-socialized dog

This dog feels secure in many everyday situations and the reinforcers and aversives reflect this.

PREFERRED REINFORCERS (1 = favourite, 5 = least favourite)

Reinforcer	Effect on dog
1 Chicken	Eats rapidly
2 Socializing with other dogs	Plays then rests - repeats
3 Chasing a thrown ball	Chases, picks up, returns to owner - repeats
4 Being touched by people	Rubs closer to people
5 Happy-sounding voice from owner	Makes eye contact and approaches owner

POSSIBLE AVERSIVES (1 = most aversive, 5 = least aversive)

Aversives are not to be used in training, but awareness of these is essential so that they can be avoided.

Aversive	Effect on dog
1 Being told 'No'	Lowers body to floor, ears flattened back against head
2 Sudden movement nearby	Flinches away and turns to source of movement
3 Dogs unfamiliar to this dog	Backs away temporarily before investigating
4 Traffic	Moves away to futher edge of path
5 Strong smells such as washing powder	Moves away and sneezes

that will hold out and fight with another to maintain your resources, or are you more likely to let another take them? A puppy coming into a home with an adult dog already in place will quickly learn his priorities; perhaps the older dog values food very highly but is not bothered about toys. As a result, the puppy will learn not to approach the adult when food is on offer, but may confidently pull a toy from the adult dog's mouth. (This is known as context-specific learning.) Humans also need to watch and learn, so they can come to understand how their dogs value their resources differently and are more protective of some than others.

If your owner seeks help for your behaviours, a dog trainer would work to assess what motivates you and then use this to help alter the course of any undesirable behaviour. Understanding that the value of resources is based on subjective judgement; a trainer will carefully monitor your responses to a variety of resources and work out your priorities. She or he can then use these, humanely, as motivational stimuli to teach you ways to act that are preferable to your owner.

Some puppies love nothing more than to run and jump into their owner's arms, while others seek out the company of other dogs or prefer quiet companionship.

Uncertain behaviour, under-socialized dog

This dog feels insecure in many everyday situations.

PREFERRED REINFORCERS (1 = favourite, 5 = least favourite)

Reinforcer	Effect on dog
1 Chicken	Eats rapidly, gulping and snatching
2 Chasing a thrown ball	Will chase but takes ball away to chew it
3 Escaping a 'threat' (such as unfamiliar dog or human; any noise near dog)	Rapidly flees any possible threat to reach safer distance in order to feel happier
4 Looking out of front window	Barks and becomes excited at passers-by, chasing along windows
5 Chews	Will not relinquish these to anyone

POSSIBLE AVERSIVES (1 = most aversive, 5 = least aversive)

Aversives are not to be used in training, but awareness of these is essential so they can be avoided.

Aversive	Effect on dog
1 Being told 'No'	Growls, barks, lunges at human
2 Sudden movement nearby	Flees or may turn and attack source of movement including dogs or people
3 Dogs unfamiliar to this dog	Barks frantically, adopts defensive body posture
4 Traffic	Lunges and barks frantically attempting to chase (or chase away) each vehicle
5 Children	Backs away and hides. If children reach out, may bark and lunge

Living with other dogs

Do you need to have the companionship of other animals? This varies from dog to dog, but for many dogs home life does involve living with other dog breeds and other species, such as cats. This section looks at the ways that you are likely to interact with other dogs and animals in your new family.

As a domesticated animal, you will spend your time in a mixed social environment. This means that not only do you share your home with humans and possibly other species, but even your fellow dogs may not be related to you directly. This means they could be very different in size and inclinations to you, and you will have much to learn about them, in terms of their values, priorities and behaviours in general. You and they may also be neutered, which means that your human owners would be wrong to make comparisons between you and feral or free-ranging dog populations when considering how you may get along together.

There are many ways in which you will seek to interact with those around you. Some of these stem from social behaviours that are described as 'neotenic' or infantile: these are play behaviours that continue into adulthood, even after sexual maturity. For instance, you may vocalize to interact with others – dogs bark and yap their whole lives, whereas young wolves and other canids lessen their vocalization as they age. Recently scientists have begun to study barking behaviours to see if they are used for carrying explicit intent.

Sometimes your communication with other dogs is relevant to your work. Hunting dogs raised together, such as Beagles or Otterhounds, allow useful observations of shared signalling in the pursuit of common prey.

The company of friends

Dogs are also observed to nuzzle and elicit care and attention using their noses or paws. These social behaviours may be mostly directed to those in your immediate family group. Whether such traits were deliberately selected is uncertain, and it is important to remember that although you are capable of such social acts with your family, you may not wish to play or interact with other dogs. Just as your owner may not be the life and soul of the party, you may prefer only those dogs that you know well. You may not welcome the bouncing Labrador charging towards you in the park, or you may be that bouncy dog, not noticing that others might not want to join in your game. You have been observed to choose preferred playmates, even from puppyhood. Your owner must recognize that you, too, have social preferences.

Hunting hounds such as Beagles, Bloodhounds and Dachshunds follow a trail by scent then indicate the direction of the prey to other dogs by baying.

GROUP DOG INTERACTIONS

When you meet other dogs, you may decide to play gently or boisterously.
You might not wish to interact and might stay away. Their responses to you will dictate how long
and how involved this social experience becomes. Not all dogs want to join in with the crowd.

On the surface

Here, five dogs appear to be enjoying a game together. Owners can learn to 'read' their dog's body language and should be prepared to step in and prevent any extreme behaviours such as a fearful, aggressive or predatory response as these can lead to damage. How might an owner learn to read these body signals? (see below)

This Boxer is standing quite stiffly and in a stalking posture, leaning his head and shoulders slightly forward. He may be following the black dog in the background or approaching the small dog in the centre. Either way his body signals show forward intent.

This dog appears not to wish to interact. He is not making eye contact and is walking in parallel to the group. He is panting which may indicate stress, or that he is hot from running or playing beforehand.

The terrier is pouncing with front feet raised. His ears are held back but his mouth is relaxed and open.

The white dog is retreating and turning away, with a high tail carriage. The interaction between this dog and the small Jack Russell Terrier suggests they may be taking turns to play and chase.

Dogs as teachers

You not only learn by interacting with your environment and your owner – you also learn from the other dogs around you. If one of you suddenly notices a sound, you will quickly start to pay attention, too. Modelling your behaviour on that of other dogs is known as 'allelomimicry'.

Allelomimicry is defined as 'performing the same behaviours as others within a short space of time', and this kind of synchronized behaviour can be seen in many species. For instance, a bird bathing in a dusty hollow will quickly be joined by others. It is a form of social learning that might be used to explain why your behaviour is not as exemplary as usual when you are among unruly friends.

You have a natural, instinctive inclination to emulate others, because it is far more efficient to learn in this manner than through simple trial and error. As a puppy, if you live with an older and more experienced dog, you may observe him going outside to toilet. You follow and perform the same deed. This makes training simpler for

your human family too. Unfortunately, an older dog that regularly toilets indoors may also be rapidly copied by the puppy, causing twice as much trouble for owners.

Adult dogs have been observed to offer modelling behaviour in an attempt to boost confidence in youngsters. For instance, a puppy that was fearful of descending stairs was seen to copy his mother who appeared to deliberately demonstrate that the steps did not represent a threat.

Amplifying other's responses

You may not always copy other dogs, but your learning can be improved by their response. This 'social facilitation' refers to the increased excitement you may feel when the dogs around you are aroused. A good example of this is in the dog competition sport of flyball, where a dog racing alongside you will encourage you to become more excited and to race faster. The increased state of arousal represents an amplification of your current response directly related to that of the other dog next to you.

This can lead to a description of 'pack mentality' within groups of dogs, whereupon the shared social response is vastly escalated. It can occur innocuously in an urban street, where a passing hot-air balloon surprises a single dog who barks, triggering all the neighbouring dogs to also bark in unison. It can also lead to over-stimulation and can escalate unwanted behaviours resulting in situations where a group of dogs attack in unison; directing these attacks towards other animals, dogs and even humans.

Dogs are affected by the behaviour of other dogs around them and will often copy each other's behaviour.

LEARNING FROM OTHER DOGS

Dogs have an innate inclination to be with other dogs and follow their lead.
This means they will notice and copy the behaviour of the dogs around them.

Learning new skills

If a dog cannot see how to access a bin, it may witness another dog climbing up onto a box to make foraging in a dustbin possible. The first dog then copies the second and succeeds.

Gaining confidence

If a puppy that is reluctant to descend steps then witnesses the parent dog descending some steps, it may copy the older dog's confident behaviour and learn how to do it.

Learning reactions

If two dogs are walking together along a street and one begins to bark at a specific type of dog (such as one that has black fur), the other dog may bark the next time he sees a black dog too.

Learning fears

If an older dog falls into a hidden ditch at some point, he may decide to avoid that area in future. Any puppy accompanying this older dog in the same area would learn from the older dog's avoidance that the ditch represents a risk and avoid it too.

Playtime with other dogs

The purpose of your play is not always clear. As a puppy it may be social rehearsal, where you learn about interacting with others, and as an adult, play may continue into mating. Or it may be a reenactment of a natural instinct; chasing after toys may reenact part of the predatory chase sequence.

Your owner may sometimes worry that you are fighting rather than playing. Increasingly loud vocalizations during inter-dog play range from squeaking noises to sharp barks and even growling as the game continues. The intensity may escalate until one of you interrupts the interaction, after which both of you may find your bodies shaking (as if wet) as you settle back down.

Signs of play

Play between dogs is recognizable from your body movements. A 'play bow' (see right) can be an invitation to begin or continue play. You may place your paw up on the other dog's shoulder, or may begin to mouth or 'play bite'. When the other dog joins in, your jaws may grip one another. Such jaw-wrestling behaviour is performed without force.

Younger or adolescent dogs learn from their interactions with others, and may not control their physical play well. Over-enthusiasm can lead to squabbles, even though there was no intention to harm. As a dog, you are likely to judge the amount of force you use by the reaction of your playmate. It is often stated that a puppy may hear a playmate shriek if one player uses too much power, signalling for play to stop. Subsequently, and as a result of the game ending in the past following a shriek, you will learn to use less force in future. However, on occasions, the shriek and rough play may stimulate the player to continue once aroused. Indeed, there is anecdotal evidence to suggest that some dogs enjoy and seek out rougher, more confrontational play. An older dog may indulge in self-handicapping, 'asymmetric' play, where they deliberately scale down their play intensity to match the skill and strength of the younger dog. You may not pull your tug toy as hard when playing with a puppy, compared to how strongly you yank on it in games with your owner. You show tolerance when a puppy attempts to play with you, as he grabs and tugs on your ears. However, this does not preclude your gently moving away, pinning him with your paw, even growling at him to teach him that he is showing too much force.

In an inviting 'play bow' you will lower the front half of your body towards the ground in a frozen posture.

PLAY BEHAVIOURS

Older dogs are often surprisingly tolerant of puppies, and healthy interactions can bring a strong sense of companionship while also teaching the puppy vital socialization skills.

Lying down to play

An older dog will often lie down to invite a puppy to play, rather than standing over the younger, smaller companion. The older dog may paw at the puppy from this supine position, allowing the puppy to set the pace for the play. The puppy can also come and go at will as he builds confidence. These important lessons teach the pup that other dogs can be gentle and friendly. Undersocialized pups may not learn this and develop coarse play styles as a result.

Playing gently

An older dog can often overpower a puppy, taking possessions straight out of the puppy's mouth if he so wishes. However, often this is not what occurs, as the older dog is more likely to attempt to initiate a tugging game. For the game to continue, the adult dog pulls more gently to encourage the pup to join in. The nature of 'healthy' play is a balanced approach; neither dog takes advantage of the other. This gives play its uniquely rewarding and teaching quality.

Recognizing that playtime is over

Owners need to recognize that the playful, give-and-take nature of the two interactions above is very different from a situation where an older dog is attempting to rest or take a peaceful nap. In this case the puppy should be gently moved away and distracted elsewhere. Being a puppy babysitter is very tiring for an older dog and if the puppy is allowed to constantly seek play, the older dog will become irritable. If play growling becomes louder or movements become rapid, it is time for a break.

Showing your feelings

Every animal can experience a range of emotions, from deepest and contented relaxation through to sheer panic. You may not be able to describe your feelings in words, but your body language can be assessed and decoded into emotions that a human can understand.

Emotive words such as 'happy' may not be accurate descriptions of how you experience emotions, but using these kinds of words may help your owner to understand and empathize more effectively with your reactions. Your emotions can change from moment to moment, just as your body movements can transition from one to another smoothly – and both of these depend on your level of arousal. An escalation of arousal can sometimes lead to over-excitement or anxiety, or even aggressive behaviour. For this reason it is very important for your owner to be able to identify the differences between these flowing states and how to make you feel more at ease, ensuring any unpleasant feelings/behaviours are avoided.

Signs of homeostasis

When you are feeling relaxed and in a state of homeostasis, or balance, your head will be up and your ears will lack tension. Your tail may be wagging gently, your eyes will take on their normal shape and your gaze is soft (see opposite, top). When alert and happy, you may elicit play by doing a play bow (see page 138) tapping your paws, and drawing back your mouth slightly while panting excitedly. You may even bark in a 'yap'.

When you are feeling slightly conflicted – perhaps excited at being reunited with your owner, but also slightly overwhelmed by the situation – you may show more 'appeasement-like' body language. Here your ears are back, your mouth relaxed and your eyes look upwards from a bowed head. You may lick your lips a little, but are not experiencing extreme arousal.

Worried and tense

When you are feeling more uncertain, you may attempt to avoid situations while being careful not to create any kind of excitement in others. Your body gestures are slow but steady, and you may attempt to withdraw. Your tail will be lowered, your front paw raised, and your ears pushed back tightly against your head. Your eyes will narrow. You may avoid eye contact with others. At times you may shake off the tension, acting as if your fur is wet when it is not. Humans need to learn not to approach you when you demonstrate these signals. To continue, and ignore such body language, can cause your emotions to escalate into a more severe, overt threat response.

Very unhappy

When very unhappy, your ears are held tightly back against your head or they may rotate sharply forward as you begin to consider repelling the threat that is apparent to you. You may lie down, cowering and frantically attempting to roll over. You may urinate. If pushed further, you may show your teeth, stiffen and growl. Your eyes may stare either directly at the potential threat, or stare into space. Your body is very tight and tense. While your body may still be leaning back, it is likely that you will suddenly start to project your body forward as you defend yourself. If your soft growling goes unheeded, you may snarl more loudly as your lips are drawn back from your teeth (but note that not all dogs growl). If such warning signs go unheeded, snapping and biting will eventually follow.

BODY TALK

You communicate using vocalization and your body language. Some of the ways you act mean different things in different contexts, so your owner needs to notice what all the different parts of your body are doing.

Happy dog

When you look like this, you pose no immediate threat to the people or animals around you.

Your head is up and your ears are held in their 'neutral' position without tension. You will have a relaxed facial expression.

Your tail may be wagging gently from side to side, and not held stiffly. You may perform a 'play bow', indicating you want to play.

When you are feeling two things at once, you may show more 'appeasement-like' body language: ears are back, mouth relaxed; eyes looking upwards but head slightly lowered.

Worried dog

When you are stressed or nervous, you will exhibit some of the behaviours shown below.

Your tail will be lowered and perhaps may start to tuck underneath your body. The more tensely the tail is tucked, the higher the level of uncertainty and stress.

Your mouth will be closed and tense, or may be panting frantically. You may even drool a little, lick your lips in a flickering motion, and may yawn.

Your front paw may be raised as the tension builds. This is particularly likely if you have a favourite toy or food item you are trying to keep for yourself.

Very unhappy dog

If you feel severely under threat, you will exhibit appeasement or aggressive behaviour.

You may begin turning your head, perhaps while bobbing or lowering it, and averting your eyes from the perceived threat.

Your tail will become tucked between your legs, and you may even perform a 'stomach flip', rolling over to indicate you are withdrawing from interaction.

If pushed further, you may show your teeth, and may stiffen and growl. Your eyes may stare either directly at the potential threat, or stare into space.

8
UNDERSTANDING HUMANS

Most dog fossils have come from human burial sites,
indicating a long-term relationship with humankind.
Parts of your evolution hint at the ways in which you have
adapted to become a valued companion, with a good
understanding of humans and their lifestyles.

Your human family

You share many of your social systems with humans. You live in families, look after your young for extended amounts of time and will even share the parenting of other young that are not directly related. Unfortunately this sometimes leads humans to mistakenly believe that you think like them.

Your family structure is not that of a rigid hierarchy; it is a more fluid and complex structure based on individual needs and relationships. Your relationship with humans mirrors this pattern and your responses to them indicate this type of affiliation.

While humans know that you are not a person, and certainly not a child, they sometimes refer to you in ways that indicate they think of themselves as your carer or 'pet-parent'. Research shows that they refer to your thought processes in a similar way to that of humans, as though perhaps you think in similar ways to them. In addition, you take on the human-assigned identity of 'dog', which has certain associations and makes humans think of you and your kind in particular ways and with certain expectations – especially about who you are and how you should think and behave. This can be unhelpful when you behave in ways that are natural to your species but that do not fit into your human's schema or model of how you 'should' be. This kind of thinking can be especially obstructive when such rigid expectations apply to your particular breed.

Understanding people

You, on the other hand, are very good at understanding humans and do not approach them with the same ideas about what a human 'should' be like. You have some useful cognitive skills to help you notice how they act and learn from your interactions with them.

Using eye-tracking technology, experimenters have been able to investigate your response to following the

Many humans expect that their dogs will like the things that they do - like being hugged - which many dogs experience as feeling trapped or threatened.

human gaze. In one innovative study, dogs were spoken to in an engaging manner before the experimenter then looked in a specific direction. The dogs indicated that they were following the experimenter's gaze by also looking in that direction. This was then compared to trials where the experimenter spoke in a non-engaging way; the dogs were not seen to follow the gaze direction (Teglas *et al.*, 2012). Such exciting evidence of collaborative activity with humans has been compared to reactions shown by six-month-old children. It seems you are aware of our intent to communicate with you.

HUMAN-DOG MISUNDERSTANDINGS

The human predisposition to understand the reaction of animals as similar to their own in any given situation means that there is often a huge gap between what the human thinks is happening inside a dog's mind and what is actually happening. Common misundertandings are listed here.

Human	Dog
Thinks their dog likes to be hugged.	May feel trapped or threatened when hugged.
Thinks their dog must play with all other dogs.	May prefer to pick and choose his friends.
Thinks their dog is playing when boisterous.	Could be scaring and overwhelming other dogs.
Thinks their dog is 'stubborn' when the dog refuses to do something.	Dog may be reluctant or scared, or ill if refusing to do something.
Thinks their dog is disobedient because the dog does not follow commands.	Dog may not have been thoroughly trained and may not understand.
Is annoyed when their dog barks (and wants a dog that does not bark).	Barking is a form of communication unique to canines. Dogs bark for lots of important reasons.
Expects their dog to be contented for hours when left alone (perhaps while the human goes to work).	Dogs are social creatures and need regular social interactions.
Finds the idea that their dog may eat rubbish or excrement disgusting.	Dog enjoys the smell and taste - it may still seem like food to them.
Does not want their dog to chase people or other animals.	Dogs are predators and still retain an excellent natural hunting ability.
Thinks a puppy should know not to damage possessions or urinate in the house.	Puppies are young animals and need to be taught how to adapt to human rules.

What family do you need?

Your owner may say that you chose them, by running up to them on the day they first saw you. In truth, you have no choice over which humans decide to take you home and it is important that your owners are prepared to provide you with the kind of lifestyle you need for happiness and wellbeing.

New owners should take into account both their own needs and those of the dog when making their choice.

Life expectancy differs widely among dogs, which is perhaps unsurprising given the enormous variation in breed type, and it should be taken into consideration by any new dog owner. A dog's lifetime is popularly expressed in 'dog years' – commonly estimated at seven to any one 'human year' – but this is inaccurate because a dog's most accelerated maturation occurs during their first year or two, but then growth slows and settles.

People can reach a better estimate of where you stand along your own lifeline by considering details about your size and breed. It is estimated that a 3½-year-old dog of any size is equivalent to a 30-year-old human, with age comparisons diversifying after this as breeds over 40 kg (90 lb) age the most rapidly.

You will need exercise whatever the weather, and active dogs need longer walks. The amount of exercise you need may not be related to your size, as some giant breeds need less exercise than a more active, smaller dog, such as a medium-sized Border Collie. Smaller dogs may fit into smaller spaces, but certain small breeds, such as terriers, can be high-energy dogs and should not be considered a less-energetic option.

Looks or personality?

Your owner may decide on a particular breed type, and their preference is often based largely on appearance. People often express a dislike for certain breeds, based on assumed characteristics that the breed is said to have. However, it has been indicated that there are more differences in characteristics within any single breed than there are between breeds.

In 2012, UK psychologists Lance Workman and Jo Fearon carried out research with the Kennel Club into correlations between dog breeds and owners' personalities. They studied seven Kennel Club categories: gun dogs, hound dogs, pastoral breeds, terriers, toy breeds, utility breeds and working breeds. The study found that people did choose dogs that they thought were 'like them'. The owners of pastoral and utility breeds were found to be the most extroverted among the owners, while the most 'agreeable' and conscientious people chose gun dogs and toy dogs (the owners of toy dogs were also the most open to new experiences). The study concluded that human personality types are attracted to certain dog breeds.

OWNERSHIP FACTORS

When choosing a dog, people need to take into account many factors, but especially those shown on the graphic below. The lifetime cost of looking after a dog may be anything from £15,000–30,000 ($21,000–43,000) depending on food bills and veterinary care.

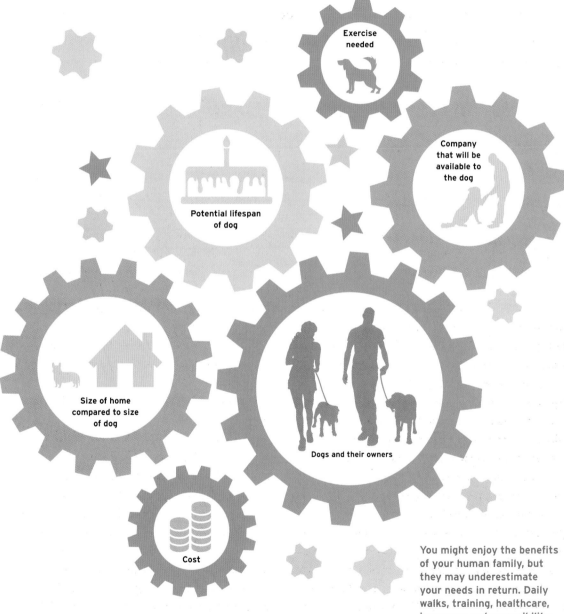

Exercise needed

Company that will be available to the dog

Potential lifespan of dog

Size of home compared to size of dog

Dogs and their owners

Cost

You might enjoy the benefits of your human family, but they may underestimate your needs in return. Daily walks, training, healthcare, insurance and reponsibility for your behaviour can be unmeasured costs.

Working for humans

You may be a 'professional' dog, working in a role that makes use of your particular size, excellent vision or hearing, or your hunting or protective skills. Such abilities may place you into a role as a stock herder, a guide or physical assistant, guardian or racing participant.

If you play a working role in your life with your owner, you will have been selected for characteristics you display rather than for your looks – although your looks may assist your ability to do your job. For example, flock-guardian dogs such as the Kuvasz, originating from Hungary, are said to have a light-coloured coat to enable shepherds to differentiate them from predators such as wolves or bears, which are prevalent in that country. The Komondor, which carries out similar tasks, has a corded coat that allows it to blend in with the sheep it protects.

The value of working dogs

Dogs are often selected for working roles that can't be carried out by people or machines, or where these may be too costly to employ. Australian livestock guardian dogs (LGDs), such as Maremma sheepdogs, are estimated to provide high value compared to the owners' original investment because of the way they protect the animal stock from predators. Such economic measures can seem a little mechanistic, as if you have no purpose other than working for human profit, but your welfare is held in the highest regard and it could be argued that your function is to perform these tasks, rather than sit in an apartment waiting for an owner's return.

If you are an assistance dog, you must behave reliably, because it is your job to provide mobility and independence to blind and partially sighted people. The UK's Guide Dogs for the Blind charity estimates that it costs around £50,000 ($70,000) to support, breed and train a dog throughout its working life, which is expected to be around seven years. The initial training of a guide dog takes 20–24 months.

Working dogs such as sheepdogs are able to exercise their natural traits – such as herding – in a way that benefits themselves, their owner and the flock they guard.

WORKING DOGS

Some dogs work as professionals in highly trained jobs, using their unique instincts as part of the wider society. Humans make use of their sociability, sensitivity to scent and awareness of movement across a range of jobs. These dogs may have been bred specifically for such skills over many generations, and their skills are perfected through extensive training.

Emergency-service dogs (such as Belgian Malinois). These dogs help the military, police and fire services in many ways, including detecting unexploded bombs.

Detection dogs (such as German Shepherds). These dogs have an acute sense of smell and a notable ability to communicate their findings to their human handlers.

Service dogs (such as Labrador Retrievers). Often bred specifically for their role, these dogs help guide humans who cannot see or hear, and assist with physical tasks such as fetching a phone or pulling open doors. They attract the attention of their owner using touch.

Livestock dogs (such as Border Collies). These dogs assist with the movement of livestock from place to place, separating off individuals from the group perhaps for veterinary treatment, and guarding them from predators such as wolves or bears. These dogs have very keen eyesight.

Hunting dogs (such as Springer Spaniels). These dogs are trained to detect, track and retrieve game. The main hunting breeds are Terriers, Hounds, Retrievers and Spaniels.

Relaxing and sharing

As you relax on your owner's lap or curl up in your bed at home, you feel safe and contented. The feeling is mutual. Owners report that pet ownership makes them happy and improves their lives. Scientists attribute some of this feeling of wellbeing to the mammalian hormone oxytocin.

When you gaze into your owners' eyes, they experience a surge of a hormone known as oxytocin, which plays a role in many behaviours including maternal bonding, pair bonding and social recognition. Oxytocin is known as the ultimate 'feel-good' hormone; it is produced in mammals in the hypothalamus region of the brain then secreted by the posterior pituitary gland.

A hormone for wellbeing

When human parents gaze at their babies, the child's oxytocin level rises, causing the baby to gaze back at the parent, thereby increasing his or her oxytocin levels. This

The feel-good hormone oxytocin is released in you and your owner when you have moments of eye contact.

means that both parent and child feel better as a result of their interaction, so the 'feel-good loop' helps to create a strong emotional bond between the parent and child.

A 2015 research study by a team of animal behaviourists at Azabu University, Japan, found evidence of a similar feel-good loop between humans and dogs. When female dogs were given oxytocin (usually through a nasal spray) their gazing behaviour towards their owners increased. Owners then looked back in return, forming a behavioural loop that appears to be mutually rewarding. This form of gentle gazing was found to provide more stimulation of oxytocin levels than talking or petting; both male and female dogs had a 130 per cent rise in oxytocin levels, while owners' levels soared by 300 per cent. Sharing eye contact appears to make both participants feel good. If further evidence were needed that dogs are a very different species to wolves, it has been shown that wolves do not show this response, even when they have been raised by humans.

Increased trust

Dogs given oxytocin in situations of apparent threat appeared to respond more readily, so the hormone seems to do much more than simply improve mood. It appears to affect a dog's awareness of social situations. In a study by biological scientist Jessica Oliva in 2015, dogs given a nasal spray of oxytocin became more trusting and cooperative, and were better able to understand social cues from their owners about the location of hidden food than a control group given a simple saline spray. When

EFFECTS OF OXYTOCIN

HUMAN

DOG

Triggers

Oxytocin is released during human childbirth and during breast-feeding. Moments of social and emotional attachment (such as looking at one another) also trigger its release. Dog owners have been shown to have increased oxytocin release when gazing at dogs with whom they have formed an emotional attachment.

A brood bitch will release oxytocin during labour and when feeding her puppies. Its release can decrease the activity of the hypothalamic-pituitary-adrenal (HPA) axis, reducing the stress response. Oxytocin levels increase after dogs engage in affiliation with other familiar dogs; the view is that social interactions also stimulate its release.

Effects

Oxytocin appears to have an anti-anxiolytic effect, reducing anxiety. It has been shown to increase empathy with others as well as playing a role in the development of romantic attachment. It promotes relaxation, trust and psychological stability, working alongside other hormones and neurotransmitters in the body and brain.

Oxytocin plays a significant part in social bonding between animals. It can also modulate stress, has a positive impact on affiliation, including mutual trust and pair bonding. Dogs administered with a nasal spray of oxytocin showed increased positive behaviours not only towards their conspecifics, but also to their human family members.

you are in training class, and your instructor asks your owners to 'get eye contact', this may be because their gaze is known to trigger oxytocin release and help you to learn. A study by Japanese animal behaviourist Takefumi Kikusui and his colleagues in 2009 found that male and female dogs experienced a 130 per cent rise in oxytocin levels after gazing into their owners' eyes. Dogs of all ages, regardless of specific training, have also been found to follow their owners pointing gestures more accurately after eye contact. Even young dogs were capable of following this brief directional gesture, suggesting that this link is something you establish at a very early age.

Influencing humans

You have a positive influence on human behaviour in many situations, but particularly in therapeutic environments, where you have been found to contribute marked psychosocial benefit. You can prevent ill-health, aid recovery and even predict changes in your owner's health.

Your contribution to human health matters may seem to be a modern development, but in fact animals have been used in this way for hundreds of years. In the 18th century, the Quaker William Tuke noted that patients in his asylum for patients with mental disorders appeared to benefit from the presence of animals and birds kept in the grounds. Florence Nightingale, in her 1859 book, *Notes on Nursing*, commented that patients confined to rest enjoyed the presence of a bird in the same room.

Beneficial health effect

Adults and children undergoing treatment for illness have been reported to benefit from visits from dogs. A 2015 study by Amy McCullough, National Director of Humane Research and Therapy for the American Humane Association, showed that visits by therapy dogs to patients in hospitals resulted in stabilizing blood pressure and heart rates in patients compared to a control group.

The long-term health of pet owners appears to gain benefits from their relationship with their pets. Pet owners have been observed to require fewer visits to healthcare providers for ailments, and dog and cat owners demonstrate fewer physical ailments (such as colds, minor allergies and headaches). A 1991 study by James Serpell, Professor of Animal Ethics and Welfare in Pennsylvania, USA, demonstrated a highly significant reduction in minor health problems among new dog owners during the first month, which was still apparent 10 months later at the end of the study.

Dogs have been shown to have a significant effect on the wellbeing of hospital patients following a welcome visit.

Detecting illness

Your special abilities go even further than this. Hypoglycaemia (low blood sugar) can cause seizures, coma and even death, but dogs can detect life-threatening blood-sugar fluctuations in humans. A medical-detection dog is trained to follow the blood-sugar levels of their owners by smelling the owner's breath. If the levels go beyond the trained parameters, the dog will signal an alert by rousing the owner or family, and fetch the essential medical kit.

Dogs can be used to detect other diseases too. Cancer cells, for instance, release small amounts of volatile substances. Dogs can be trained to detect such substances and to indicate to humans when they (and therefore cancerous cells) are present.

HEALTH DETECTION BY DOGS

Some dogs are trained specifically for detecting or responding to a particular kind of human disease or condition, and will react in a way that brings vital help to the human sufferer, by fetching medical aid and/or immediate human assistance.

Cancer
Detects scents of volatile organic compounds from urine or breath samples to detect cancer.

High/low blood pressure
Detects changes and can prevent patient fainting from sudden undetected drop in blood pressure.

Diabetes
Detects changes in blood-sugar levels through changes in volatile organic compounds through pores.

Panic and anxiety disorders
Learns signals of anxiety. Provides social support in public and general companionship. Prevents isolation.

Seizures
Recognizes and warns of impending seizures (trained response). Remains with human to assist with aftermath of a seizure.

Your extraordinary scenting ability means that you can smell changes (in skin or body products such as urine) that humans are unable to detect. You are trained for a minimum of six months for these tasks.

Deafness
Alerts to sounds, such as the telephone or doorbell.

Other conditions
Fetches medical kit. Alerts others of patient's distress.

Blindness and impaired vision
Sees possible hazards. Steers safe routes.

Elderly needs
Picks up items, opens doors, fetches the telephone, empties the washing machine, carries bags.

Playing with humans

You and your owner probably enjoy playing together, but your play styles will take many differing forms. For play to continue, both you and your owner must find it beneficial. If the unspoken rules are not followed, the game will end, so you need to find a way to understand each other.

Several studies examining human–dog play interactions have shown that people and dogs employ a series of specific 'give and take' rituals and invitations. These play signals are similar to those found in the field of human developmental psychology; specifically, they follow a 'call and response' pattern. As a dog playing with a human, you'll find yourself matching the human in terms of intensity and type of behaviour, playing in parallel.

Come and play

In 2000, Dr Nicola Rooney *et al.*, found that when dogs play with a human, rather than another dog, they are more likely to initiate play projects that are more interactive and less competitive. They were also found to offer a game object to their owners more quickly than they would to another dog. Vocalization by humans was

Certain postures, such as this body crouch with a toy or hand slapping the ground, are attractive play signals.

found to help considerably in beginning play with dogs, but they were able to recognize and respond to many body signals accompanied by sounds, especially the play bow and lunge. It's likely that you and your owner both invite play by slapping hands (or paws) down on the floor and making sudden pawing or reaching movements.

Games for dogs and people

Fetching games are characterized by a human showing and throwing an item, such as a toy, then a run to retrieve it. You and your owner may take turns to retrieve the toy, sometimes pursuing the item or racing alongside one another in a chase.

Possessive games are those that involve playing with the possession of toys. For instance, your owner may put his or her hand out to take your toy while you stay just out of reach. You may occasionally relinquish the toy, or choose to retire to another location to investigate the toy further by chewing it.

Chasing games involve you or your owner becoming involved in a chase. These games end when one of you becomes physically tired or over-stimulated. In this state, you may be tempted to grab or tackle the other participant (your owner).

You may like rough and tumble games, like wrestling with your owner. This may include light or heavy physical contact, and rolling on the floor in feigned combat. You may mouth and bite your owner without force, and you may growl and vocalize. This game will end if excessive force is used.

FUN GAMES FOR DOGS

If your owner can't take you outside to play for any reason, you will enjoy these games, which engage mind and body.

'Chase me!'

In chasing games with your owner it is possible for you to become over-stimulated. Biting your owner may signal that the game needs to end.

Rough and tumble

Some games involve an element of rough and tumble, which you enjoy. If you begin to use excessive force it is a signal for the game to end.

Hide and seek

If your owner shows you a toy then hides it while you're out of sight, you will have great fun using your tracking skills to find it.

'Fetch!'

Games of Fetch draw upon your natural instinct to hunt and retrieve. The act of fetching also means that the game can play on.

Come and play!

Humans have developed ways of inviting you to play, which might include slapping hands on the floor or simply calling you with outstretched arms.

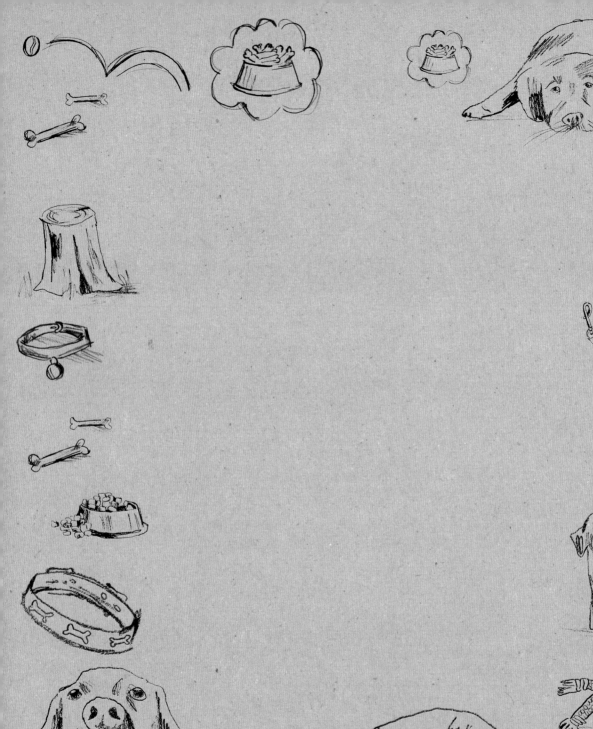

9

THE AUTUMN YEARS

Dogs live longer than ever before, but as you age you may begin to hear and see less well, and your appearance may alter as grey hairs appear around your eyes, on your muzzle, or even all over your body. You may no longer move with the freedom of your younger years, but you still have much to offer as a companion.

Aches and pains

Life expectancy differs widely in dogs, which is unsurprising given the enormous variation in breed type. It can be lengthened and enjoyed by a good diet, daily exercise and mental challenges. Smaller dogs often have longer lifespans, and neutering can reduce the risk of some cancers.

As you get older, just like humans, you can suffer from aches and pains ranging from mild to severe. Regular health checks with your vet will minimize the impact of such ailments on your daily life.

Arthritis may affect your joints and can cause you to walk more slowly or struggle to move as freely as when you were young.

Breed lifespans (estimated)

Breed	Average lifespan	Old age begins
Beagle	10	8
Boxer	9	7
Bulldog	6	5
Dachshund	15	12
Doberman	8	6
German Shepherd	10	8
Golden Retriever	12	9
Irish Setter	11	9
Labrador Retriever	11	9
Poodle (Miniature)	16	12
Shih Tzu	15	11
Yorkshire Terrier	15	11

Hip scores measure the general soundness of your hip and socket. However, even a healthy hip score may see joint deterioration as you age. Your owner must seek advice about pain relief at the earliest sign of stiffness or even grumpy behaviour on your part.

Your claws must be kept trimmed especially if your increasing age reduces your level of exercise.

You will be considered 'geriatric' from any age between five and ten, depending on your breed and size. A study by O'Neill *et al.* in 2013 found that the longest-lived breeds were the Miniature Poodle, the Bearded Collie, the Border Collie and the Miniature Dachshund. The shortest-lived were the Great Dane and the Dogue de Bordeaux. Crossbreeds were found to live longer lives, exceeding purebreed lifespans by 1.2 years.

Disease and ageing

Dogs, like humans, age at different rates. As this can be difficult to track, you need to attend regular checks with your vet (twice a year is recommended as a minimum). These will ensure you are kept free from disease and pain, and will pick up any developing problems so they can be treated early. Your vet is likely to carry out dental care and routine blood tests to check your overall health.

Your immune system may no longer be as robust as when you were younger, which means that you will have less defence against disease, so early treatment is essential. Like older people, geriatric pets can develop cancer, heart disease, kidney and urinary tract disease, liver problems, diabetes, joint or bone disease and senility. Arthritis or inflammation of the joints is common. Your bone surfaces are covered with cartilage, along with fluid that allows the bones to slide together without friction as you move. As you age, this cartilage can become worn or damaged and the increased friction causes discomfort and further inflammation.

Natural ageing conditions

On a hot and sunny day, you will need to remain in a shady, cooler place. If your fur becomes matted or unkempt, this may be a sign that you cannot groom yourself as efficiently as when you were younger. Your owner can help you with this, but will also ask your vet to check whether pain or discomfort from a developing condition is preventing you from cleaning yourself.

Your skin may become thinner, putting you at increased risk of damage or injury even when you are just playing. Any injuries may also take longer to heal than when you were younger. You may develop skin lumps, most of which are likely to be benign and may not need removal, but since they may be cancerous, they will all need checking.

As an older dog, your food will need to include easily digested ingredients with anti-ageing nutrients. As you may be less active, your weight will also need to be carefully monitored.

DOG VS HUMAN AGE

DOG AGE	0-9 kg (0-20 lb)	9-23 kg (20-50 lb)	23-40 kg (50-90 lb)	>40 kg (>90 lb)
	HUMAN AGE			
1	7	7	8	8
2	13	14	16	18
3	20	21	24	26
4	26	27	31	34
5	33	34	37	41
6	40	42	45	50
7	44	47	50	56
8	48	51	55	64
9	52	56	61	71
10	56	60	66	78
11	60	65	72	86
12	64	69	77	93
13	68	74	82	101
14	72	78	88	108
15	76	83	93	115
16	80	87	99	
17	84	92	104	
18	88	99	109	
19	92	101	115	
20	96	105		
21	100	109		
22	104	113		
23	108	117		
24	112			
25	116			

Early years
Adult-Middle age
Middle age-Senior
Senior-Geriatric

Ageing brain and senses

Your vision, hearing, and sense of touch and smell may deteriorate as you age. You may experience less detail in your surroundings as a result and could become slower in your responses to events and changes in the external world. You may begin to sleep very deeply.

Older dogs generally experience deterioration in hearing and sight, and may develop specific eye problems. Nuclear (or lenticular) sclerosis can appear in dogs over six years of age; this shows in the eyes as a whitish or blueish haze. The extent to which this will affect your vision will vary from dog to dog. It is caused by the compression of older lens fibres as new ones develop, and it is the increased density of the lens that causes it to look cloudy. Cataracts in the eye will also cause a similar cloudy look and these can cause inflammation and blindness, even in younger dogs.

Mental agility

Now that your senses are not as sharp, you may startle more easily, for example when people approach you, because you may not have heard or seen them from afar. You might also be less responsive to situations and may fail to recognize friends you previously adored.

Canine cognitive dysfunction is a form of dementia that affects just over 14 per cent of dogs; less than 4 per cent of dogs aged eight years or over showed symptoms, so diagnosis is difficult. Your owner may notice that you are behaving differently, such as showing signs of disorientation or acting in repetitive, abnormal ways. You may stand and stare into space or walk in circles from time to time. You will respond a little slower when called for your dinner or to go for a walk.

Commonly these symptoms are similar to separation-related disorders; in both cases you may bark at night and panic when alone. You may even bark in fear at objects in the home that you no longer seem to recognize. Your previously unblemished house-training record may change overnight as you lose control over toileting and no longer ask to go outside. Your behaviour may vary from day to day, so an overall picture of your health may provide the best clues for diagnosis.

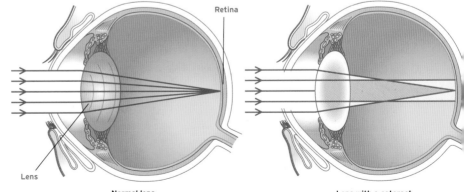

A cloudy eye may be a result of ageing or indicate a more serious complaint such as a cataract. When the eye's lens clouds over, it is unable to focus light on the retina and vision becomes blurred or dimmed as a result.

Retina

Lens

Normal lens

Lens with a cataract

CHECKLIST: CANINE COGNITIVE DYSFUNCTION

Your owner can use this chart to record their observations of your behavioural changes as you get older.

Symptoms or signals	Date/time observed	Duration of behaviour
Reversal of routine (day routine at night time and vice versa)		
Becoming disorientated in familiar places		
Staring at walls or into space for long periods		
Bumping into corners or doorways		
Barking and vocalizing at night		
Distress at separation, day and night		
Barking for no obvious reason		
Easily startled by previously familiar events		
Failing to recognize family and friends		
Loss of appetite or forgetting they have just eaten and demanding a meal		
Forgetting pre-trained signals such as 'Sit!'		
Repetitive behaviours such as circling or air licking		
Pacing, which may be accompanied by panting, without obvious cause		
Toileting in the house in front of owners when used to ask to go outside		
Reduced enthusiasm to leave the house		
Sleeping for longer periods during the day compared to past behaviour		
Becoming more fearful and reduced engagement in everyday activities that were once routine		

Keeping happy in old age

Veterinary practices report seeing an increasing number of senior dogs, so they have become much more familiar with treating them. They can also teach your owner how to manage the multiple conditions that you may experience in old age. Luckily, your life experience helps you stay calm and happy.

Even in old age, you are still able to learn new skills and may find that you are calmer than younger dogs, because you have plenty of life lessons behind you. You'll have developed your own personality, learned how to get along with people and fit in with human lifestyles, and will have long outgrown your puppy-based need for chewing important human accessories such as slippers.

Easy companions

Older dogs make great companions for older people, because they enjoy sitting still for long and enjoyable petting sessions, and they will stay by someone's side when going for walks in the park, rather than wanting to run off and play. They may be more tolerant of children too and less reactive than younger dogs. Older dogs do not need as much stimulation or training as younger dogs, making them very rewarding pets for busy people as well. A happy older dog, it turns out, can make a lot of humans very happy too!

The family elder

As you age, your owners may decide to add a younger dog to the household. The energy and interest of a companion dog will be entertaining for you, but only if the puppy is well-managed by the humans who care for you. Puppies have lots of energy in short bursts, allowing you to share quality time with your owners when the puppy is resting. Your owners need to make sure you have access to a comfortable area that is well out of reach of the puppy, so that you can retreat when the puppy begins to pull on your ears or over-tire you. This maintains a balanced and enjoyable mutual relationship.

In good health, your golden years are often relaxed, enjoyable years of gentle companionship.

Young puppies can rejuvenate an older dog, but expecting you to 'parent' a puppy is too much; it can be exhausting.

10 WAYS TO EASE OLD AGE

Even with the sensory difficulties that old age brings, you can still enjoy an excellent quality of life.
Your owner must consider what you find comfortable and fun now, rather than looking back at your youth.
This outlook means that your needs can be fully met, even if you are not as active or aware.

As an elderly dog, you will benefit from stimulation in short bursts as well as physical supports to help you rest and move around easily. You may have retired, but your brain is still active and you will appreciate this special kind of attention.

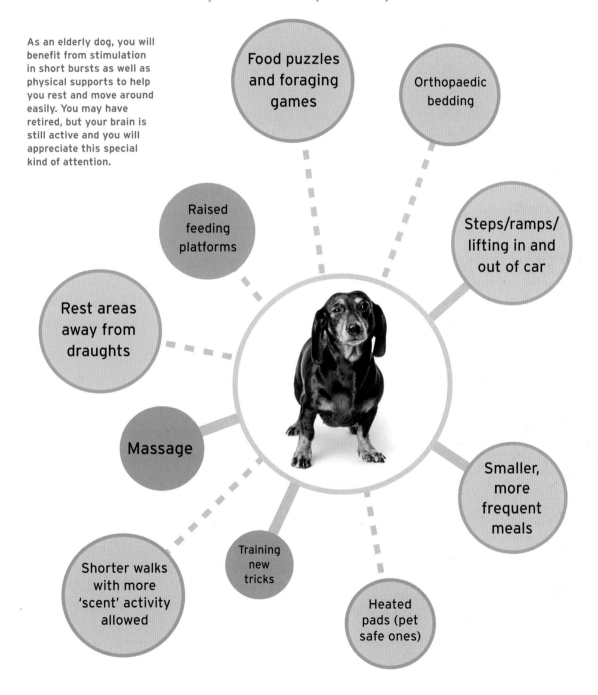

Food puzzles and foraging games

Orthopaedic bedding

Raised feeding platforms

Steps/ramps/lifting in and out of car

Rest areas away from draughts

Massage

Smaller, more frequent meals

Shorter walks with more 'scent' activity allowed

Training new tricks

Heated pads (pet safe ones)

Time to say goodbye

We have no way of knowing whether you have any concept of death, but there have been several famous cases of dogs appearing to grieve over the deaths of their owners. You are also likely to be affected by the death of other dogs in your family, because of the loss of their companionship.

Just as owners form attachments with dogs, and dogs with their owners, it is likely that they also form attachments with other dogs in the family. In instances where puppies have been raised and trained as pairs, they have been observed to show distress when one of their pair leaves the other, even for a short time or over a short distance. If you are used to being part of a family that has several dogs, the loss of one of those animals will – at the very least – have an impact upon your daily routine. Not only will your owner indicate upset at the loss, your steady companion will no longer be available as before.

Can a dog 'know' that its owner is in a particular grave? Certainly dogs notice their lifelong companion has gone.

The loss of people affects you too: there are many stories of dogs who waited patiently at their owner's graves, seemingly unwilling to leave them. They may have shared a great deal of time together, particularly if the owner was elderly or worked with the dog. If a dog has provided vital emotional support, both the dog and person will have felt the strength of this emotional bond.

As a dog, you are adept at adjusting to new events, but for a short (or sometimes long) period following an owner's death, you may show signs of distress. This can be alleviated by your remaining family giving you plenty to do, such as taking you for walks, playing games with you and offering you tastier food for a temporary period, so you are encouraged to eat. Dogs also enjoy learning, so positive-reinforcement based training will raise serotonin levels. This natural chemical boosts brain-cell communication related to mood, appetite and sleep.

A more comfortable death

Research indicates that the sudden or unexpected death of a dog or cat can lead to prolonged grieving in your human owners, especially where there was a high level of attachment. However, many dogs experience a slower, longer-anticipated death, where their owners eventually come to realize that their dog's level of chronic pain, cognitive dysfunction or severe impairment in day-to-day functioning means that euthanasia may be advisable. A vet will guide them in making this kind of decision, using an assessment scale to consider all aspects so that everyone is clear if or when this is the kindest option.

QUALITY OF LIFE CHECKLIST

Your owner can use this chart when potentially difficult decisions may need to be made. They simply need to decide upon a score for each section (1 is low and 10 is high) and then add the scores together.
A total of 35 points or more means there is an acceptable quality of life.

Score	Criterion
1-10	**HURT** Adequate pain control, including breathing ability, must first and foremost be considered. Is the dog's pain being successfully managed? Is oxygen supplementation necessary?
1-10 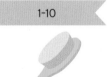	**HUNGER** Is the dog eating enough? Does hand feeding help? Does the dog require a feeding tube?
1-10	**HYDRATION** Is the dog dehydrated? For dogs that are not drinking enough, use subcuraneous fluids once or twice daily to supplement fluid intake.
1-10	**HYGIENE** The dog should be brushed and cleaned, particularly after elimination. Avoid pressure sores and keep all wounds clean.
1-10	**HAPPINESS** Does the dog express joy and interest? Is the dog responsive to things around him (such as family and toys)? Is the dog depressed, lonely, anxious, bored or afraid? Can the dog's bed be close to the family activities and not be isolated?
1-10 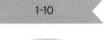	**MOBILITY** Can the dog get up without assistance? Does he need human or mechanical help (such as a cart)? Does the dog feel like going for a walk? Is he having seizures or stumbling?
1-10 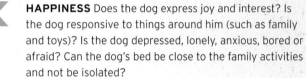	**MORE GOOD DAYS THAN BAD** When the bad days outnumber the good, quality of life might be compromised. When a healthy human-animal bond is no longer possible and a dog is suffering, a decision needs to be made.

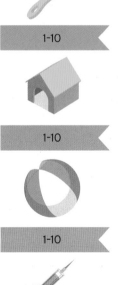

Adapted from *Canine and Feline Geriatric Oncology: Honoring the Human-Animal Bond*, by Alice Villalobos and Laurie Kaplan, with permission.

10
PROBLEMS YOU MIGHT FACE

You are likely to experience health and behavioural problems
from time to time. These situations are inconvenient when
they occur from time to time, but occasionally the entire
relationship between you and your owner may reach
a crisis point and require immediate attention.

Travel troubles

Your owner may expect you to accompany them on journeys and holidays – around a quarter of UK dog owners say they have changed holiday plans so that their pet could accompany them. However, the noise, smell, unfamiliarity and motion of a vehicle may have a unpleasant impact on you.

Many dogs travelling in cars find themselves strangely stimulated by the sights whizzing past their window. Some sights are stationary (such as the car seat) while some are moving past (such as the roadside). The conflict between sight and spatial orientation can cause serious motion sickness in many animals. The vestibular system, which controls balance and spatial orientation, and involves the inner ear, sends one set of information to the brain. The ocular system, involving what you see, transmits visual information to the retina that in turn also travels to the brain. If the information from these two systems conflict in the brain, the resulting mismatch results in nausea, particularly when a dog's body is exposed to accelerations of movement in different directions, as happens when travelling. In scenarios like this you may start to salivate, become very still, or pant and pace frantically.

As a adult dog, you may find that you feel anxious when travelling. This may stem from previous trips as a puppy, where the separation from your litter coupled with the unfamiliar, noisy and fuel-scented environment felt slightly threatening. This form of travel anxiety can build into a serious phobia and may require professional treatment from a vet or behaviourist.

An anxious traveller

You need to be physically secure when travelling, for legal and safety reasons. Unfortunately around 20 per cent of dogs in the UK have been found to travel in the back seat of a car without any form of restraint. This would make

Some dogs jump in the car quite happily, while others may be more reluctant and anxious travellers.

you and other passengers vulnerable if the car were to stop suddenly or crash: an unrestrained 4.5 kg (10 lb) dog involved in a crash at 30 mph would exert roughly 136 kg (300 lb) of pressure onto anything it collided with, according to the AAA Foundation for Traffic Safety in the USA. It is essential that all dogs are secured inside a moving vehicle, either with appropriate harness and seat belt or behind a secure dog guard.

MOTION SICKNESS

Motion sickness occurs when there is a discrepancy in visual stimuli (what the dog sees) and the stimuli perceived by the inner ear's balance organ. Motion sickness is more common in puppies and young dogs because the ear structures are not yet fully developed.

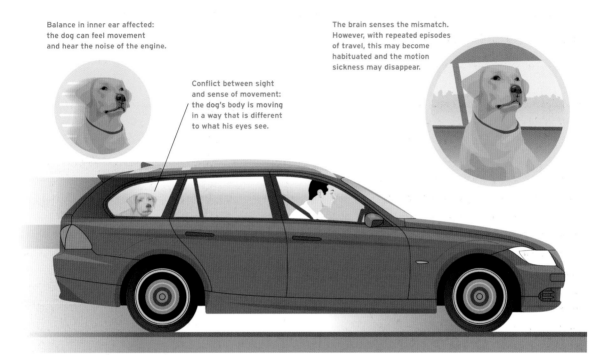

Balance in inner ear affected: the dog can feel movement and hear the noise of the engine.

The brain senses the mismatch. However, with repeated episodes of travel, this may become habituated and the motion sickness may disappear.

Conflict between sight and sense of movement: the dog's body is moving in a way that is different to what his eyes see.

Safer transport

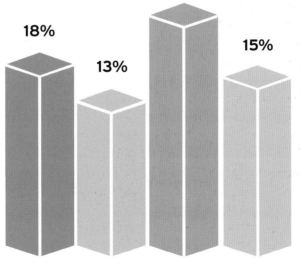

Around 18 per cent of owners that are familiar with the Animal Welfare Act say that their dog is safely secured on the back seat of a car, while of owners who are unfamiliar with the Act, only 13 per cent secure their dogs.

18%

13%

20%

15%

Around 20 per cent of dogs in the UK are transported in cars on the back seat without a seatbelt. Only 15 per cent travel either in the boot (behind a dog guard) or on the back seat with a seat belt.

Don't leave me

Dogs are social creatures, so it is easy to see why you might feel distressed when left alone. Some dogs are so badly affected by experiences of isolation that they begin to behave anxiously when they think it may recur. This may even lead to them trying to stop their owners from leaving the home.

If a dog is going to suffer from attachment issues, it is likely to experience the onset of separation anxiety before three years of age. While some elderly dogs do begin to experience these symptoms for the first time, these are usually found to be a sign of cognitive dysfunction (see pages 160–61).

Isolation distress

The PDSA (People's Dispensary for Sick Animals) PAW report of 2015 noted that 28 per cent of dog owners believe it is acceptable to leave a dog home alone for 6–10 hours a day. This means that in the UK, more than two million dogs are left alone for five hours or more on a weekday. Signs of distress at being left alone include vocalization (barking and howling), pacing, toileting and distressing physiologial symptoms such as rapid heart rate, panting, dilation of the pupils, and possibly extreme emotions, such as panic. For a dog left alone, a disturbance outside the home such as deliveries being made may be upsetting. Boredom may also lead to unwanted behaviours. It is recommended that you are not left for more than four hours per day if you are a mature dog, and less time than this if you are a puppy.

Since you learn by associating events, you can easily predict when you are likely to be left alone. Some owners say that their dogs behave anxiously when the thought of leaving has only just crossed their mind. This occurs because the owner's 'departure cues' may be minutely demonstrated body signals which are nonetheless easy for a vigilant dog to notice. Some dogs do not react to being left by their owner if another human being is present, while others become distressed at separation from their owner even when other people are present. Your owner may get another dog to keep you company but if you are attached to a specific human being, this will do little to help you feel better.

Some dogs learn to predict their owner's departures and wait anxiously for their return.

SIGNS OF DISTRESS

The following are sample symptoms of distress that may be shown when a dog is left alone for several hours at a time. The symptoms are often best observed using video camera. Any or all of these may be visible, but the more symptoms there are, the more severe the condition, as they provide evidence that the dog is experiencing severe stress. A dog in this situation may attempt to reunite with its owner, damaging doorways and window exits in the process. This usually occurs within the first half an hour of being left.

Signs of increasing separation anxiety

Mild	Moderate	Extreme
Pacing	Barking continuously	Chewing paws or flanks
Climbing up on tables and other furniture (by a dog that would not normally do this)	Howling	Self mutilation in attempts to escape/exit/reunite with owner
Chewing or sucking fabrics, such as bedding, rugs, etc.	May specifically attach to one owner; will show symptoms when this owner is not present even if other humans/dogs are present	Vomiting
Barking - intermittent	Panting rapidly	Defecation, diarrhoea
Very enthusiastic greeting upon owner returning, even after a very short while	Excessive consumption of water	Urination
Follows owner around the house but may settle while owner is in other rooms	Follows owner constantly, seeking continuous physical contact and attention	Extreme, incessant destructive behaviour
Ignores favoured, tasty food or chews when owner absent	Constant anxiety when left; no relaxation observed	'Shut down' - severe withdrawal from everyday situations
May show signs of anxiety when owner leaves but this is temporary and dog can relax	Exhaustion when owner returns and excessive sleeping	Excessive shedding of fur
		Biting of fur (bald patches without other medical cause)
	May persistently refuse to leave doorway where owner is attempting to exit	Aggressive behaviour (often in an attempt to prevent owner leaving)
	May show signs of 'learned helplessness' by retiring to his bed but remaining anxious	Drooling/dribbling (pools of saliva may be seen, dog may be very wet around mouth/chest)

Frustrated and bored

You try to show your human family what you need by repeating certain actions, and in this way you gradually school them in understanding and supporting your needs. However, when your needs are not met, you may experience frustration, which can lead to aggressive behaviour.

If you suffer from social isolation, such as being left home alone while your owner works or you are living in kennels, this reduces your ability to indulge in certain healthy behaviours such as play. Some dogs seek this activity more than others, but it is believed to be a fundamental, innate need in animals.

The need for play

Failure to provide opportunities for socializing can lead to despondency, and the urge to interact may increase over time. In some animals, such as rats, young

Some dogs play more energetically and aggressively when reunited with other dogs after a time alone.

animals that have been isolated for a few hours are found to play with exceptional enthusiasm in rough-and-tumble games when reunited, which are initiated within just a few seconds of meeting. Your owner might be surprised to realize that the way you roughly leap up at them or bulldoze your dog friends may in fact be a simple and direct result of your being left alone. If on any occasion you are left alone to the point of becoming frantic, you may redirect your frustration onto any nearby dog or human that ventures near you.

Other ways that dogs show their frustration and boredom are by scratching and chewing furniture, barking, howling, shredding books and newspapers, and – if they are outside – running up and down continually or digging holes in the garden. All of these are attempts to tell their owner that they are bored and need something or someone to play with.

Sickness and boredom

Post-operative recovery requiring minimal exercise or 'cage rest' will turn your regular routine upside-down, and you will suffer from a lack of mental and physical activity. Your owner may not realize the impact this can have and will be acting on veterinary advice not to over-exercise you, so might be surprised to learn that even during physical recovery periods you need some gentle stimulation. For planned surgery, your owner can introduce you to a crate beforehand and provide new enrichment toys for activity (see pages 122–23), to stop you from becoming bored.

DEALING WITH FRUSTRATION

Play with me again!

1
ACTIVITY IS OCCURRING
A dog engaged in a fun activity will enjoy it.

2
ACTIVITY STOPS
When the activity stops, the dog will be less happy – most dogs will realize the activity depends on their owner and begin to find ways to restart the activity.

3
ESCALATED ATTEMPTS
A dog who really enjoys the activity may begin to use increasingly obvious behaviours to try and tempt the owner back into the game. This may include barking, pawing and scratching, hyperactive behaviour, rough play, or aggressive behaviour.

Cycle of anger

Triggering event

Emotional (internal) response

Intensification and amplification

External response (barking, scrabbling)

Behaviours peak (explosive)

Exhaustion

Withdrawal/ adaptive phase

When unable to meet your needs, a specific trigger may generate a frustrated, 'angry' response. This then intensifies and manifests externally with explosive behaviours, leaving you tired and withdrawn until the next trigger occurs.

Aggressive behaviour

Can you feel anger? In dogs, aggressive behaviour is typified by a particular head and body stance, which may be defensive or offensive in nature. It can be defined by the context in which it occurs, as it is an attempt to prevent another animal from continuing a course of action.

In 2012, the UK's Association of Pet Behaviour Counsellors noted that 65 per cent of primary reported problems with dogs involved aggression towards dogs and people. Within this, 36 per cent were behaving aggressively towards people, including animal professionals such as groomers and vets; 29 per cent of dog problems involved aggressive behaviour towards other, unfamiliar dogs.

All dogs are capable of aggressive behaviour should they be unable to cope with a situation.

If you perceive that another dog is trying to take a bone from you, you may attempt to stop this by lunging, growling, barking, snapping or biting. This may not necessarily mean that you feel 'angry', but it is clear that you are feeling uncomfortable and are using force to re-establish your feelings of safety or possession. In this way, aggressive behaviour can be understood as a standard part of every animal's repertoire.

Speed and intensity of response

The two questions of most importance to your owner in these situations are 'how readily do you offer aggressive behaviour to deal with a situation?' and 'how much force do you show in the first instance?' You may experience different levels of tolerance to stress compared to other dogs, but in all cases, if a dog perceives a threat to continue, then its stress levels increase. Escalation of stress leads to physical and psychological distress that can result in aggressive or self-destructive behaviour. Body signals show signs that you are uncomfortable (see pages 80–81) and illustrate how you are feeling. You may try to avoid the situation, or you may force the situation to stop through growling, lunging or biting.

If you show these forms of behaviour, it is essential that you receive a veterinary check to ensure you are not ill or in pain. Your owner can then seek professional help from a Certificated Animal Behaviour Counsellor.

THE DOG BITE SCALE

Veterinarian and animal behaviourist Ian Dunbar formed this chart for assessing the severity of biting problems as a way of gaining an objective evaluation of the danger posed by a dog who has bitten a human.

Level 1

Obnoxious or aggressive behaviour but no skin contact by teeth.

Level 2

Skin contact by teeth but no skin puncture. However, there may be skin nicks and slight bleeding on person caused by forward or lateral movement of teeth against skin, but no vertical punctures.

Levels 1 and 2 comprise well over 99 per cent of dog incidents. The dog is certainly not dangerous and more likely to be fearful, rambunctious or out of control. There is a very good prognosis for this dog, as the problem may be quickly resolved with basic training, especially classical conditioning and numerous repetitive Come/Sit/Food reward sequences, progressive desensitization handling exercises and numerous bite inhibition exercises and games.

Level 3

1-4 punctures from a single bite with no puncture deeper than half the length of the dog's canine teeth. The bite may show lacerations in a single direction, caused by victim pulling hand away, owner pulling dog away, or gravity (as might occur when a little dog jumps, bites and drops to the floor).

The prognosis for this dog is fair to good, provided that the owner does everything that a professional trainer recommends. However, treatment is both time-consuming and not without danger. Rigorous bite-inhibition exercises are essential.

Level 4

1-4 punctures from a single bite with at least one puncture deeper than half the length of the dog's canine teeth. May also have deep bruising around the wound (dog held on for a number of seconds and bore down) or lacerations in both directions (dog held on and shook its head from side to side).

This dog is very dangerous. Prognosis is poor because of the difficulty and danger of trying to teach bite inhibition to an adult hard-biting dog and because absolute owner compliance is rare. The dog should be confined to the home at all times (except for visits to a vet, with muzzle in place). It must only be allowed contact with adults; whenever children or guests visit the house, the dog must be confined to a single locked room or roofed, chain link run with the only keys kept on a chain around the neck of the owner. All bite incidents must be reported to the relevant authorities (animal control or police).

Level 5

Multiple bite incident with at least two Level 4 bites or multiple attack incident with at least one Level 4 bite in each.

This dog is extremely dangerous and mutilates. It is simply not safe around people. However, the quality of life is so poor for dogs that have to live out their lives in solitary confinement that euthanasia is recommended.

Level 6

Victim of attack killed.

Reproduced with the kind permision of Dr Ian Dunbar

Afraid and anxious

Anxiety is a physiological, psychological and behavioural state that is induced in animals when they are confronted with a severe threat to their wellbeing or survival. Many physiological changes take place in your body, which are designed to help you deal with the threatening situation.

If you are prompted into a state of extreme fear, your body will react by activating a particular response in the autonomic nervous system, in readiness for fight, flight or freeze (like a rabbit caught in car headlights). Once in this state, you will notice many changes in your physiology: your heart rate will speed up, you may drool or vomit, and begin to tremble. Your pupils will dilate to help you focus more keenly.

The situations in which these responses will come into effect depend upon many things, including genetic influences on your temperament, your early experience and socialization as a puppy, and any learning you have gained from unpleasant incidents. For instance, if you once experienced a treatment as extremely painful at the veterinary surgery, you may go into a fight/flight/ freeze response on your following visits. In addition, it is thought that dogs enter a second fearful phase (sometimes known as the second 'fear impact' period) during their adolescence, so at this age your sensitivity will be heightened.

Trigger and response

Fear manifests itself under many circumstances. It could be that you have not experienced a stimulus before, and it startles you. For example, a lorry loudly racing past as you and your owner walk along the nearby path. During this first occurrence, you experience a fear response, but there is a consequence for the future too, because now you may anticipate the frightening lorry whenever you walk along that path.

Your activated response of fight, flight or freeze depends on the most efficient survival response at the time. For instance, your owner may see you freeze completely, as animals do in the wild when they try to avoid being seen by predators. Alternatively you may flee, so that you can avoid the threat by running away from it. Or you may remain in place but fidget, scratching yourself frantically or chewing at your paws. Aggressive behaviour or 'fight response' is often used as a means to drive a threat away. This does not mean you have a predisposition to behave in this manner. Animals may demonstrate all of the above, only resorting to aggressive behaviour when all other attempts to cope have failed. On future occasions, you will simply choose the most effective option when this situation last occurred, which means that if aggression seemed to be the answer, you are likely to repeat a form of aggressive behaviour.

You may flee when faced with a threatening posture, in order to reach a safe distance from the perceived threat.

THE FEAR RESPONSE

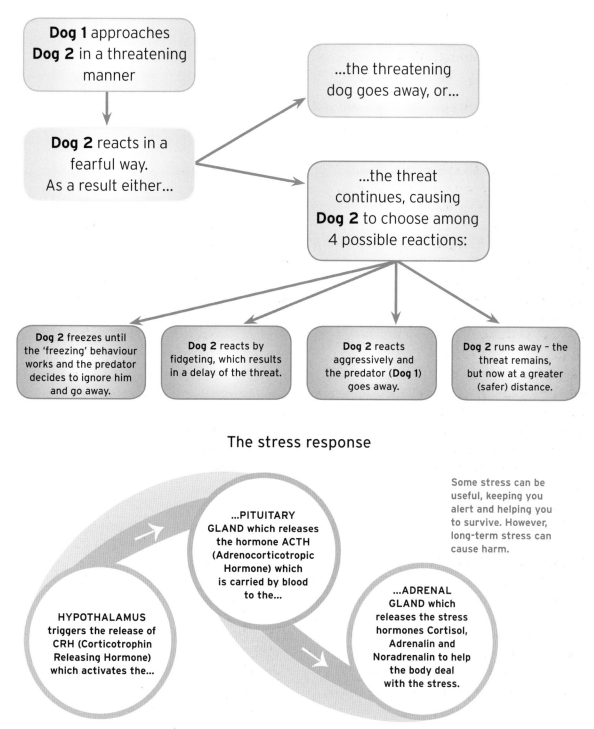

Dog 1 approaches **Dog 2** in a threatening manner

Dog 2 reacts in a fearful way. As a result either...

...the threatening dog goes away, or...

...the threat continues, causing **Dog 2** to choose among 4 possible reactions:

Dog 2 freezes until the 'freezing' behaviour works and the predator decides to ignore him and go away.

Dog 2 reacts by fidgeting, which results in a delay of the threat.

Dog 2 reacts aggressively and the predator (**Dog 1**) goes away.

Dog 2 runs away – the threat remains, but now at a greater (safer) distance.

The stress response

HYPOTHALAMUS triggers the release of CRH (Corticotrophin Releasing Hormone) which activates the...

...**PITUITARY GLAND** which releases the hormone ACTH (Adrenocorticotropic Hormone) which is carried by blood to the...

...**ADRENAL GLAND** which releases the stress hormones Cortisol, Adrenalin and Noradrenalin to help the body deal with the stress.

Some stress can be useful, keeping you alert and helping you to survive. However, long-term stress can cause harm.

Dogs and children

You are likely to come into contact with children throughout your life. Understanding the nature of this interaction and assessing the risks of your contact with children is an essential part of dog ownership, so your owner will be keen to see what socialization skills you already have.

Dogs that are unfamiliar with children may be startled by their smaller size, higher-pitched voices and sudden, fast movements. Children learn to show affection by hugging, kissing and touch, but these actions could appear threatening to you, even though they are well-meant. Natural childlike behaviours such as running, yelling, grabbing and darting about – especially while maintaining eye contact with a dog – may put them at increased risk.

This is because these behaviours may excite or surprise a dog, causing them to bite, which may account for the large proportion of children who are bitten by dogs each year. A 2001 report by the American Veterinary Medical Association on human-canine interactions found that 335,000 people in the USA are admitted to hospital for dog bites every year, and children under 12 account for around half of these admissions.

Natural childlike behaviours and curiosity can seem threatening to you.

Vulnerable when young

Younger children are more likely to be bitten by dogs (of any size or breed) that are already familiar to them. The bites are more likely to occur in their home and are inflicted around the child's head and neck area. The most common age group for children suffering this kind of dog bite is three to seven years. Older children and adults are more at risk of bite injury to their limbs. This difference may be due to the way that younger children like looking at the dog's face as a way of interacting, often placing their own faces nearby.

Learning to play

While you can become used to children's noise and activity levels, your owner will need to closely supervise all your interactions with children. By assessing the levels of enjoyment or discomfort you display at varying intensities of play, your owner can keep both you and any child safe, and guard against either you or a child from being injured.

GETTING TO KNOW YOU

The companionship that children and dogs can mutually provide is important, but can cause confusion at times, because humans show affection and happiness in different ways to dogs. As a result, adults must never allow children to have unsupervised access to dogs.

Being kind

You show affection by licking and snuggling, but a child may not enjoy this. Children may think you like to be kissed and hugged, but this may make you feel trapped.

Playing games

Hide and seek is an enjoyable game for you to practise finding your human family. Care must be taken that play does not become rough or over-excitable as this can lead to injury.

Going for walks

Even if a child's own dog is well-behaved, other dogs they meet may not be well-trained. Walks should always be supervised by an adult.

Training tricks

Training is a positive, enjoyable way for both children and dogs to learn how to interact safely, with rules that they both understand.

Other scary things

Dogs that suffer from anxiety and fear do not live as long as those with less stress in their lives, so it is very important for your owner to recognize the situations that make you feel nervous and help you through them. Repeated occurrences of high fear levels may lead to post-traumatic stress disorder.

Modern-day fears and phobias can be many and varied. You may not enjoy being around the vacuum cleaner or lawn mower. These are noisy devices, spewing out hot air, dust or grass clippings, so your urge to get away from them is understandable. Your hearing is already more sensitive than that of your owner, so the rotation of the metallic shafts within the motor can give off a deafening screech that humans cannot hear to the same extent. To add to the sensory insult, vacuum cleaners appear to lunge forward and then retreat; in the natural world this is interpreted as a threatening form of behaviour. Even if your owner is sweeping with an innocuous broom, this motion alone may cause you to attack it to keep it at bay.

You may view the lunging movement of a vacuum cleaner as threatening and take refuge under furniture.

Canine PTSD

Fireworks are unexpected, loud, explosive sounds, which not only cause the air to vibrate but can be sensed through the floor. Extreme reactions to fireworks can cause dogs to suffer long-term consequences, and they may find daily life increasingly difficult as they anticipate the threat returning and so feel under constant stress. Canine Post-Traumatic Stress Disorder (C-PTSD) is a reported phenomenon in military dogs, who display stress and anxiety symptoms that continue far beyond situations of immediate threat.

Where a dog has suffered excessive trauma, their learned response can extend into their everyday life, causing them to constantly feel under threat; this can dramatically affect their health and potentially reduce their lifespan. C-PTSD can also occur in dogs who have been roughly treated or abused in training, consistently threatened, or have experienced trauma in a situation that is out of their control, such as a car accident, hurricane or earthquake.

Punishment pitfalls

In the past, dog training often involved punishment of a harsh nature, such as yanking a dog's neck using a slip lead or choke chain, or pushing on its back end to make it sit. Even in modern times people have been known to use a sharp spiked device known as a 'prong collar'. Electric-shock collars are now widely available although they are illegal in some countries, including Denmark, Sweden, Norway, Austria, Switzerland and Germany.

When painful punishment is added to a situation, a dog learns to associate the situation with pain and so avoids the situation in future to avoid repeated episodes of pain. This method of training often looks successful because the dog stops reacting when it occurs, but it is highly problematic. Studies have shown that devices such as choke chains cause physical harm, such as damage to the throat and eyes.

In addition, a dog may not realize what caused the human to issue the punishment, so it may learn to associate the pain with something other than the thing intended, such as people approaching. If so, the next time people approach, the dog might try to flee or become aggressive to prevent the predicted punishment occurring. Dogs are likely to stop trusting (and may come to fear) the person issuing the punishment.

WHAT ARE YOU AFRAID OF?

A wide range of things are reported to make you feel uncomfortable or afraid. This can be resolved with thorough early socialization and gradual positive experience by pairing with enjoyable things such as treats.

	Dogs	Cats
Vacuum cleaner	28%	60%
Fireworks	39%	39%
Loud noises	26%	42%
Unfamiliar people	14%	37%
The vet	19%	29%
Thunder and lightning	25%	22%
Travelling in the car	8%	33%
Other dogs/cats	13%	17%
Traffic	7%	19%
Having ears/eyes/feet examined	11%	12%
Children	3%	18%
Other animals	4%	15%
Having teeth brushed	8%	9%
Being groomed	7%	7%
Being left alone at home	9%	4%
None of the above – my pet is not afraid of anything	20%	10%

The development of severe fears and phobias occurs through a combination of genetic factors and early experiences, especially level of socialization and habituation to noisy and unusual environments.

Figures taken from The People's Dispensary for Sick Animals (PDSA) Animal Wellbeing (PAW) Report 2015.

Predatory problems

As part of your natural predatory instinct, you are attracted to fast movement and high-pitched squealing sounds. It is what makes playing with your squeaky toys so rewarding and chasing them gives you vital exercise. You may grab the item and shake it, as you might when killing a rabbit or rat.

Dogs are predators, who move through the same defined set of actions as wolves when it comes to finding and consuming prey. The sequence is triggered by the movement of prey, and follows this order: Orient, Eye, Stalk, Chase, Grab-bite, Kill-bite, Dissect and finally, Consume (see opposite). Domestic dogs rarely reach the Kill-bite, Dissect or Consume stages, and this may be a result of suppression through selective breeding. Certain aspects of the sequence are more evident in some breeds; for example the Pointer will point and fix, stalking; the Collie or Working sheepdog with 'collie eye' will freeze and Eye (fixate), then crouch to Stalk before giving Chase.

Such 'predatory aggression' is a natural impulse as you hunt for food, but this behaviour also appears to be enjoyable to you. However, difficulties arise if your predatory response is extreme – for instance, if your enjoyment of chasing becomes hard to control. Chasing wildlife can lead you across roads in front of traffic, while chasing livestock such as cows or sheep is illegal.

Drifting from play to prey

It has been suggested that your predatory instinct can 'drift', so you may start chasing your fellow dogs in play, but end up grabbing or biting them using similar behaviour to that of larger prey, such as deer. Dogs that have injured people, especially children, may sometimes be behaving in a predatory manner, failing to recognize their victims as human family. Alternatively, they may be showing territorial aggression – in which case they will stop chasing the person once he or she leaves their territory. A dog that is acting out predatory behaviour will stalk, chase and try to attack and bite their target, regardless of the location.

Chasing wildlife is a natural behaviour for you, but can leave you dangerously out of control.

Chasing other dogs is part of your play, but can drift into predatory behaviour, causing injury from grabbing.

THE PREDATORY SEQUENCE

Dogs go through a series of transitions when hunting prey. This behaviour forms a continuum, where body signals can alter dramatically within a few seconds. Some dogs become 'fixed', such as the Pointer while orienting towards prey (as shown below).

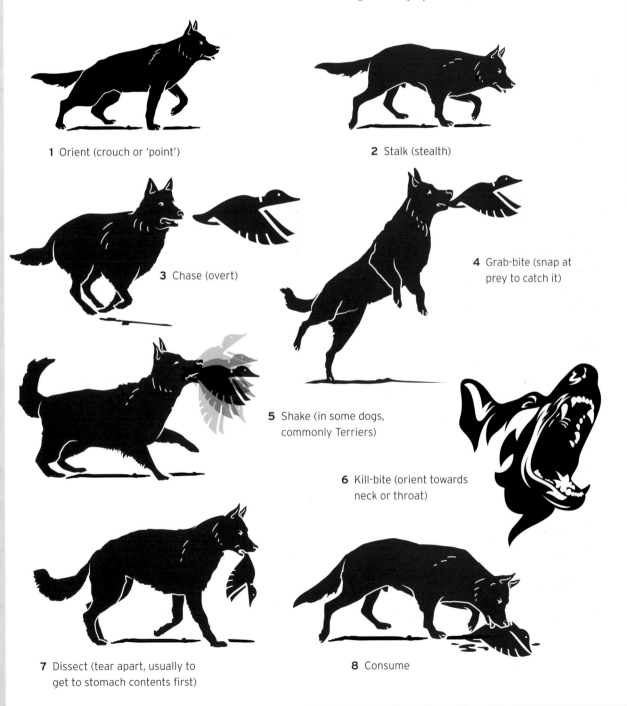

1 Orient (crouch or 'point')

2 Stalk (stealth)

3 Chase (overt)

4 Grab-bite (snap at prey to catch it)

5 Shake (in some dogs, commonly Terriers)

6 Kill-bite (orient towards neck or throat)

7 Dissect (tear apart, usually to get to stomach contents first)

8 Consume

References

pp.10-11 Being a modern dog

American Pet Products Association. (2016) *2015-2016 APPA National Pet Owners Survey.* Greenwich, CT: APPA.

Coren, S. (2012) 'How Many Dogs Are There In the World?' *Psychology Today,* published online 19 September 2012: https://www.psychologytoday.com/blog/canine-corner/201209/how-many-dogs-are-there-in-the-world (accessed 22.2.16).

Euromonitor International. (2015) Pet Care Reports on 53 countries in 2015; available online from http://www.euromonitor.com/pet-care-in-india/report (accessed 22.2.16).

Pet Food Manufacturers Association. (2014) *PFMA Pet Population Report 2014.* London: PFMA.

Richmond, R. (2013) 'Pet ownership in Australia.' *The Australian Veterinary Journal,* 91.11 (2013): N2-N2.

The American Veterinary Medical Foundation. (2012) *US Pet Ownership & Demographics Sourcebook.* Washington DC: AVMA.

The European Pet Food Industry Federation (FEDIAF). (2014) *FEDIAF Facts and Figures 2014.* Brussels: FEDIAF.

Bradley, T. and King, R. (2012) 'The Dog Economy Is Global – but What Is the World's True Canine Capital?' *The Atlantic,* online publication 13 November 2012 (accessed 22.2.16).

pp.12-13 Your lifestyle

Christian H., Westgarth C., Bauman A., Richards E.A., Rhodes R., Evenson K., *et al.* (2013) 'Dog ownership and physical activity: A review of the evidence.' *The Journal of Physical Activity and Health,* 2013; 10(5): 750-9.

Payne, E., Pauleen C. & McGreevy, P. (2015) 'Current perspectives on attachment and bonding in the dog-human dyad.' *Psychology Research and Behavior Management,* 8: 71.

Petplan (2011). *Petplan Pet Census 2011.* Published online at: https://www.petplan.co.uk/petcensus/censusinfo.pdf (accessed 22/2/16).

Rehn, Therese, *et al.* (2014) 'Dogs' endocrine and behavioural responses at reunion are affected by how the human initiates contact.' *Physiology & Behavior,* 124 (2014): 45-53.

Serpell, J. (1991) 'Beneficial Effects of Pet Ownership on Some Aspects of Human Health and Behaviour.' *Journal of the Royal Society of Medicine,* December 1991, 84: 717-720

pp.14-15 How you are built

Budiansky, S. (2000) *The Truth About Dogs: The Ancestry, Social Conventions, Mental Habits and Moral Fibre of Canis Familiaris.* USA: Viking Penguin.

Ettinger, S., Feldman, C. (2010) *Textbook of Veterinary Internal Medicine,* 7th edition. London: Elsevier.

Stonehenge. (2014) *The Comparative Anatomy of Man, the Horse and the Dog.* London: Abhedananda Press.

pp.18-19 Your Brain

Andics, Attila *et al.* (2014) 'Voice-Sensitive Regions in the Dog and Human Brain Are Revealed by Comparative fMRI.' *Current Biology,* 24.5: pp.574-78.

Dilks, D., Cook, P., Weiller, S., Berns, H., Spivak, M. & Berns, G. (2015) 'Awake fMRI reveals a specialized region in dog temporal cortex for face processing.' PeerJ 3:e1115 https://DOI.org/10.7717/peerj.1115.

Müller, C., Schmitt, K., Barber, A. & Huber, L. (2015) 'Dogs Can Discriminate Emotional Expressions of Human Faces.' *Current Biology,* 25.5: pp.601-605.

Racca, A., Guo, K., Meints, K. & Mills, D.S. (2012) 'Reading Faces: Differential Lateral Gaze Bias in Processing Canine and Human Facial Expressions in Dogs and 4-year-old Children.' *PLoS ONE* 7(4): e36076. DOI:10.1371.

Somppi, S., Törnqvist, H., Hänninen, L., Krause, C. & Vainio, O. (2014) 'How dogs scan familiar and inverted faces: an eye movement study.' *Animal Cognition,* 17: pp.793-803.

Stoeckel, L.E., Palley, L.S., Gollub, R.L., Niemi, S.M. & Evins, A.E. (2014) 'Patterns of Brain Activation when Mothers View Their Own Child and Dog: An fMRI Study.' *PLoS ONE* 9(10): e107205. doi:10.1371/journal.pone.0107205.

Vingerhoets, G., Berckmoes, C., & Stroobant, N. (2003) 'Cerebral Hemodynamics During Discrimination of Prosodic and

Semantic Emotion in Speech Studied by Transcranial Doppler Ultrasonography.' *Neuropsychology,* 17.1: pp.93-99.

pp.20-21 Your ancestors

Carles, V. *et al.* (1997) 'Multiple and ancient origins of the domestic dog', *Science,* 276: pp.1687-89.

Lord, K. (2013) 'A Comparison of the Sensory Development of Wolves (Canis lupus lupus) and Dogs (Canis lupus familiaris).' *Ethology,* 119.2, pp.110-120.

Nobis, G. (1979) 'Man Domesticated Wolves in the Late Paleolithic Age.' *Umschau,* 79: p.610.

Ostrander, E.A., Wayne, R.K. (2005) 'The canine genome.' *Genome Research,* Dec; 15(12): pp.1706-16.

Ryan, D. (2009) 'Dogs and Wolves – Different Socks in the Trousers of Evolution.' Published online by the Association of Pet Behaviour Counsellors, Oct 2009, accessed 12/10/15 (http://www.apbc.org.uk/blog/dogs_wolves)

Savolainen, P., Zhang, Y.P., Luo, J., Lundeberg, J. & Leitner, T. (2002) 'Genetic evidence for an East Asian origin of domestic dogs.' *Science,* 298: pp.1610-13.

pp.22-23 Your evolving form

Figueirido, B., Martín-Serra, A., Tseng, Z. & Janis C. (2015) 'Habitat changes and changing predatory habits in North American fossil canids.' *Nature Communications,* 2015; 6: p.7976.

Provet. (1999) 'The Dog Through Evolution.' Published online by Provet Heathcare Information at: http://www.provet.co.uk/dogs/evolution%20of%20the%20dog.htm (accessed 22.2.16).

pp.24-25 A domesticated animal

Freedman, A.H. *et al.* (2014) 'Genome Sequencing Highlights the Dynamic Early History of Dogs.' *PLoS Genetics:* 10(1): e1004016.

Savolainen, P., Zhang, Y.P., Luo, J., Lundeberg, J. & Leitner, T. (2002) 'Genetic evidence for an East Asian origin of domestic dogs.' *Science,* 298: pp.1610-13.

Shannon, L. *et al.* (2015) 'Genetic structure in village dogs reveals a Central Asian domestication origin.' *PNAS 2015:* 112 (44) pp.13639-44.

Skoglund, P. *et al.* 'Ancient Wolf Genome Reveals an Early Divergence of Domestic Dog Ancestors and Admixture into High-Latitude Breeds.' *Current Biology,* 25, Issue 11: pp.1515-19.

pp.26-27 How you lived with humans in the past

Abbott, F. (1912) *Society and Politics in Ancient Rome.* New York: Scribner's Sons.

Berlin-Brandenburg Academy of Sciences and Humanities. (1994) *Corpus Inscriptionum Latinarum,* 10.659.1-2.

Campbell, G.L. (2014) *The Oxford Handbook of Animals in Classical Thought and Life.* Oxford: Oxford University Press.

Podberscek, A., Paul, E. & Serpell, J. (Eds) (2000) *Companion Animals and Us: Exploring the Relationships Between People and Pets.* Cambridge: Cambridge University Press.

Walker-Meikle, K. (2013) *Medieval Dogs.* London: The British Library.

pp.30-31 Form or function?

Belyaev, D.K. (1969) 'Domestication of animals.' *Science,* 5.1: pp.47-52.

Spady, T. C. & Ostrander, E. A. (2008) 'Canine Behavioral Genetics: Pointing Out the Phenotypes and Herding up the Genes.' *American Journal of Human Genetics,* 82(1): pp.10-18.

Trut, L. (1999) 'Early Canid Domestication: The Farm-Fox Experiment.' *American Scientist,* 87.2: p.160.

Vaysse, A., Ratnakumar, A., Derrien, T., Axelsson, E., Rosengren Pielberg, G., Sigurdsson, S., *et al.* (2011) 'Identification of Genomic Regions Associated with Phenotypic Variation between Dog Breeds using Selection Mapping.' *PLoS Genet* 7(10): e1002316. DOI:10.1371/journal.pgen.1002316. Artwork © 2011 Vaysse *et al.* reproduced under the terms of the Creative Commons Attribution License.

pp.34-35 What can you see?

Davidson, G., Butler, S., *et al.* (2014) 'Gaze Sensitivity: function and mechanisms from sensory and cognitive perspectives.' *Animal Behaviour,* 87: pp.3-15.

Kasparson, A.A., Badridze, J. & Maximov, V.V. (2013) 'Colour cues proved to be more informative for dogs than brightness.' *Proceedings of the Royal Society B*: Biological Sciences, 280; p.1766.

Neitz, J., Geist, T. & Jacobs, G. (1989) 'Color vision in the dog.' *Visual Neuroscience*, 3 (1989), pp.119–25.

pp.36–37 Seeing near and far

McGreevy, P., Tanya D., Grassi & Harman, A. (2003) 'A strong correlation exists between the distribution of retinal ganglion cells and nose length in the dog.' *Brain, Behavior and Evolution*, 63.1: pp.13–22.

pp.38–39 Tracking motion

Miklosi, A. (2008) *Dog Behavior, Evolution & Cognition*. New York: Oxford University Press.

pp.42–43 Scent as information

Gaultier E. and Pageat P. (2003) 'Effects of a synthetic dog appeasing pheromone (DAP) on behaviour problems during transport.' *Proceedings of the 4th International Behaviour Meeting*: Proceedings Number 352, University of Sydney Post-Graduate Foundation in Veterinary Science; Sydney, Australia; pp.33–35.

Landsberg, G. M., *et al.* (2015) 'Dog-appeasing pheromone collars reduce sound-induced fear and anxiety in beagle dogs: a placebo-controlled study.' *Veterinary Record*, 2015; 177:260 DOI:10.1136.

Tod, E., Brander, D. and Waran, N. (2005) 'Efficacy of dog appeasing pheromone in reducing stress and fear related behaviour in shelter dogs.' *Applied Animal Behaviour Science*, 93.34: pp.295–308.

Young-Mee, K. *et al.* (2010) 'Efficacy of dog-appeasing pheromone (DAP) for ameliorating separation-related behavioral signs in hospitalized dogs.' *The Canadian Veterinary Journal*, 51.4: pp.380–84.

pp.44–45 A memory for scent

Bauer, N.K. (2000) *German Shorthaired Pointer*. New Jersey: Kennel Club Books Inc.

Bolan, S (2008) *The Labrador Retriever*. New Jersey: OTTN Publishing, p.92.

Cornu, J.N., Cancel-Tassin, G., Ondet, V., Girardet, C., & Cussenot, O. (2011) 'Olfactory detection of prostate cancer by dogs sniffing urine: a step forward in early diagnosis.' *European Urology*, 59: pp.197–201.

Stockham, R. *et al.* (2004) 'Specialized use of human scent in criminal investigations.' *Forensic Science Communications*, 6.3.

pp.48–49 Delicious or disgusting?

Eldredge, D., Carlson, L. *et al.* (2007) *The Dog Owner's Home Veterinary Handbook (4th edition)*. New Jersey: John Wiley & Sons.

Gwaltney-Brant, S. 'Chocolate: Food Hazards'. (2013) *Merck Veterinary Manual*. Accessed online at: http://www.merckvetmanual.com/mvm/toxicology/food_hazards/chocolate.html

Kennel Club (UK). (2016) *Common Canine Poisons in the House and Garden: Information Guide*. Published online: https://www.thekennelclub.org.uk/media/605397/poisons.pdf (accessed 1 March 2016).

Lindsay, S.R. (2000) *Handbook of Applied Dog Behavior and Training (1)*. New Jersey: Wiley-Blackwell.

Sherrington, C.S. (1906) 'Observations on the scratch-reflex in the spinal dog.' *The Journal of Physiology*, 34 (1-2): pp.1–50.

The People's Dispensary for Sick Animals (PDSA) *Animal Wellbeing (PAW) Report 2015*. Shropshire: PDSA.

pp.50–51 Sounds interesting!

Andics, A. *et al.* (2014) 'Voice-sensitive regions in the dog and human brain are revealed by comparative fMRI.' *Current Biology*, 24.5: pp.574–578.

Fay, R.R. (1988) *Hearing in Vertebrates: a Psychophysics Databook*. Winnetka IL: Hill-Fay Associates.

Heffner, H. (1983) 'Hearing in large and small dogs: Absolute thresholds and size of the tympanic membrane.' *Behavioral Neuroscience*, 97.2: p.310.

Strain, G.M. (2015) 'The genetics of deafness in domestic animals.' *Frontiers in Veterinary Science*, 2.29. DOI: 10.3.3389.

Warfield, D. (1973) 'The study of hearing in animals.' Gay, W. (ed.) *Methods of Animal Experimentation, IV*. London: Academic Press, London.

pp.52–53 Naturally sound-seeking

Altman, J. A. and Kalmykova, I.V. (1986) 'Role of the dog's auditory cortex in discrimination of sound signals simulating sound source movement.' *Hearing Research*, 24.3 (1986): pp.243–53.

Ashmead, D., Clifton, R. & Reese, E. (1986) Development of auditory localization in dogs: single source and precedence effect sounds. *Developmental Psychobiology*, 19(2): pp.91–103.

Lipman, E. A. and Grassi, J. R. (1942) 'Comparative auditory sensitivity of man and dog.' *The American Journal of Psychology*, 55: pp.84–89.

pp.54–55 Talking Dog

Dale, S. (2015). *'Dogs may not have a specific language, but they do know how to communicate.'* Published online by My Pet World, at: http://tribunecontentagency.com/article/dogs-may-not-have-a-specific-language-but-they-do-know-how-to-communicate-e (accessed 22 February 2016).

Molnár, C. *et al.* (2006) 'Classification of dog barks: a machine learning approach.' *Animal Cognition*, 11.3: pp.389–400.

Pongracz, P., Molnar, C., Miklosi, A. & Csanyi, V. (2005) 'Human Listeners can Classify Dog (Canis familiaris) Barks Recorded in Different Situations.' *Journal of Comparative Psychology*, 119.2: pp.136–44.

pp.56–57 Responding to sound

McConnell, P.B. (1990) Acoustic structure and receiver response in domestic dogs, *Canis familiaris.'* *Animal Behavior*, 39.5: pp.897–904.

McConnell, P.B. (1990) 'Lessons from animal trainers: The effect of acoustic structure on an animal's response' in Bateson, P. and Kloffer, P. (eds) *Perspectives in Ethology*. New York: Plenum.

McConnell, P.B. (2013) *'Canine Behavior and Acoustics in Shelters and Kennels.'* Published online at http://www.patriciamcconnell.com/theotherendoftheleash/canine-behavior-and-acoustics-in-shelters-and-kennels (accessed 2 March 2016).

pp.62–63 Physical responses

Gácsi, M. *et al.* (2005) 'Species-specific differences and similarities in the behavior of hand-raised dog and wolf pups in social situations with humans.' *Developmental Psychobiology*, 47.2: pp.111–22.

pp.64–65 How you learn

Greenwood, J. (2015) *A Conceptual History of Psychology: Exploring the Tangled Web*. Cambridge: Cambridge University Press.

Pavlov, I.P. (1927) *Conditioned Reflexes* (trans. Anrep, G.V.). Oxford: Oxford University Press.

pp.66–67 Learning is rewarding

Craig, A.D. (2003) 'A new view of pain as a homeostatic emotion.' *Trends in Neuroscience*, 26.6: pp.303–307.

Thorndike, E.L. (1898) 'Animal Intelligence: An Experimental Study of the Associative Processes in Animals.' *Psychological Monographs: General and Applied*, 2.4.

pp.68–69 Why did you do that?

Skinner, B.F. (1953) *Science and Human Behavior*. New York: The Macmillan Company.

Skinner, B.F. (1971) *Beyond Freedom and Dignity*. New York: Bantam Books.

pp.70–71 Working in partnership

Hare, B. and Woods, V. (2013) *The Genius of Dogs: Discovering the Unique Intelligence of Man's Best Friend*. London: Oneworld Publications.

Shipman, P. (2015) 'How do you kill 86 mammoths? Taphonomic investigations of mammoth megasites.' *Quaternary International*, 359: pp.38–46.

pp.72–73 Your memory

Clayton, N., and Dickinson, A. (1998) 'Episodic-like memory during cache recovery by scrub jays.' *Nature*, 395: pp.272–74.

Eacott, M.J., Easton, A., & Zinkivskay, A. (2005) 'Recollection in an episodic-like memory task in the rat.' *Learning & Memory*, 12.3: pp.221–23.

Lind, J., Ghirlanda, S. & Enquist, M. (2015) 'Animal memory: a review of delayed match-to-sample data from 25 species.' *Behavioural Processes*, 117: pp.52–58.

Zhou, W., Hohmann, A.G. & Crystal, J. (2012) 'Rats answer an unexpected question after incidental encoding.' *Current Biology*, 22.12: pp.1149-53.

pp.74–75 What are humans saying?

Kaminski, J., Call, J. & Fischer, J. (2004) 'Word learning in a domestic dog: evidence for 'Fast Mapping.' *Science*, 304: pp.1682-83.

Pilley, J.W. and Reid, A.K. (2011) 'Border collie comprehends object names as verbal referents.' *Behavioural Processes*, 86.2: pp.184-95.

Pilley, J.W. (2013) 'Border collie comprehends sentences containing a prepositional object, verb, and direct object.' *Learning and Motivation*, 44.4: pp.229–40.

pp.78-79 Sixth sense

Sheldrake, R. (1999) *Dogs that know when their owners are coming home: And other unexplained powers of animals.* New York: Three Rivers Press.

pp.80-81 Sensitization and phobias

Appleby, D. *et al.* (2002) 'Relationship between aggressive and avoidance behaviour by dogs and their experience in the first six months of life.' *Veterinary Record*, 150.14: pp.434–38.

Beerda, B. (1997) *Stress and Well-being in dogs.* The Netherlands: Ponsen and Looijen BV.

Guthrie, E.R. (1935) *The Psychology of Learning.* New York: Harper & Row.

pp.86-87 Being a puppy

Appleby, D.L., Bradshaw, J.W.S. & Casey, R.A. (2002) 'Relationship between aggressive and avoidance behaviour by dogs and their experience in the first six months of life.' *Veterinary Record*, 150: pp.434–38.

Appleby, D.L. and Pluijmakers, J. (2004) 'The foundations of canine behaviour' in Appleby, D.L. (ed.) *The APBC Book of Companion Animal Behaviour.* London: Souvenir Press Ltd.

Battaglia, C. L. (1995) 'Developing high achievers' (originally published as: 'Early neurological stimulation'). *The AKC Gazette*, May 1995: pp.46–50.

Gazzano, A. *et al.* (2007) 'Effects of early gentling and early environment on emotional development of puppies.' *Applied Animal Behaviour Science*, 110.3-4: pp.294–304.

McCune, S., McPherson, J.A. & Bradshaw, J.W.S. (1995) 'Avoiding problems: The importance of socialisation' in: Robinson, I. (ed.) *The Waltham Book of Human-Animal Interaction: Benefits and responsibilities of Dog Ownership.* Oxford: Pergamon.

Pfaffenberger, C.J. & Ginsburg, B.E. (1963) *The New Knowledge of Dog Behavior.* New York: Howell.

Scott, J.P. & Fuller, J.L. (1965) *Genetics and the Social Behavior of the Dog.* Chicago: University of Chicago Press.

Scott, J.P., Ross, S. & Fisher, A.E. (1959) 'The Effects of Early Enforced Weaning on Sucking Behavior of Puppies.' *The Journal of Genetic Psychology*, 95.2: pp.261–81.

Serpell, J. (1995) *The Domestic Dog: Its Evolution, Behaviour and Interactions with People.* Cambridge: Cambridge University Press.

Temple, G. and Deesing, M. (1998) *Genetics and the Behavior of Domestic Animals.* Cambridge MA: Academic Press.

pp.88-89 Mixing with friends

Appleby, D. (2010) 'Puppy Socialisation and Habituation (Part 1) Why is it Necessary?' Published online by The Association of Pet Behaviour Counsellors, (http://www.apbc.org.uk/articles/puppysocialisation1), accessed 22 February 2016.

Lehmann, V. *et al.* (2013) 'The human and animal baby schema effect: correlates of individual differences.' *Behavioural processes*, 94: pp.99–108.

Nittono, H. *et al.* (2012) 'The power of Kawaii: viewing cute images promotes a careful behavior and narrows attentional focus.' *PLoS ONE* 7 (9): e46362.

pp.90-91 Puppy behaviour tests

Battaglia, C.L. 'Early neurological stimulation.' (2008) *Journal of Veterinary Behavior*, 3.4: p.183.

Dehasse, J. (1994) 'Sensory, emotional and social development of the young dog.' *The Bulletin for Veterinary Clinical Ethology*, 2.1-2: pp.6–29.

Fox, M.W. (1971) *Integrative Development of Brain and Behaviour in the Dog.* Chicago: University of Chicago Press.

Fox, M.W. (1978) *The Dog: Its Domestication and Behaviour.* New York: Garland STPM Press.

Pfaffenberger, C.J. *et al.* (1976) *Guide Dogs for the Blind: their Selection, Development, and Training.* London: Elsevier Scientific Publishing Company.

Westgarth, C., Reevell, K. & Barclay, R. (2012) 'Association between prospective owner viewing of the parents of a puppy and later referral for behavioural problems.' *Veterinary Record*, 170.20: p.517.

pp.92-93 Puppy genetics

Battaglia, C.L. 'Early neurological stimulation.' (2008) *Journal of Veterinary Behavior*, 3.4: p.183.

Berger, C., Berger, B. & Parson, W. (2009) 'Canine DNA Profiling in Forensic Casework: The Tail Wagging the Dog.' *Forensic Science Review*, 21.1: pp.1-13.

The Kennel Club (UK). (2015) *Breeding for Health.* Published online at http://www.thekennelclub.org.uk/media/451962/breeding_health.pdf (accessed 22.2.16).

The Forensic Science Service (2004). *Guide to DNA. DNA match probability in humans.* Published online at https://www.cps.gov.uk/legal/assets/uploads/files/lawyers'%20DNA%20guide%20KSWilliams%20190208%20(i).pdf (accessed 22.2.16).

pp.94-95 Learning good habits

Dunbar, I. (2004) *Before and after getting your puppy.* Novato, CA: New World Library.

Houpt, K.A. (2010) *Domestic Animal Behaviour for Veterinarians and Animal Scientists.* Iowa, USA: Wiley-Blackwell.

pp.96-97 A healthy puppy physical

The Kennel Club (UK). *General Puppy Health: Vaccinations, Fleas & Health Checks.* Published online at: http://www.thekennelclub.org.uk/getting-a-dog-or-puppy/general-advice-about-caring-for-your-new-puppy-or-dog/general-puppy-health/#sthash.Dv1Dwd3T.dpuf (accessed 22.2.16).

pp.100-101 Adolescence

Fox, M.W. (1971) *Integrative Development of Brain and Behaviour in the Dog.* Chicago: University of Chicago Press

Scott, J.P. and Fuller, J.L. (1965) *Genetics and Social Behaviour of the Dog.* Chicago: The University of Chicago Press.

Serpell, J.A. & Jagoe, J.A. (1995) 'Early experience and the development of behaviour' in Serpell, J. (ed.) *The Domestic Dog – its Evolution, Behaviour and Interactions with People.* Cambridge: Cambridge University Press.

Shepherd, K. (2002) 'Development of behaviour, social behaviour and communication in dogs' in Horwitz, D., Mills, D. and Heath, S. (eds.) *BSAVA Manual of Canine and Feline Behavioural Medicine.* Gloucester: BSAVA.

pp.104-105 Emotion and awareness

Panksepp, J. (2003) 'Feeling the pain of social loss.' *Science*, 302: pp.237–39.

Panksepp, J. (2005) 'Toward a science of ultimate concern.' *Consciousness and Cognition*, 14: pp.22–29.

Panksepp, J. (2005) 'Affective consciousness: Core emotional feelings in animals and humans.' *Consciousness and Cognition*, 14: pp.30–80.

Panksepp, J. (2005) 'Beyond a joke: From animal laughter to human joy?' *Science*, 308: pp.62-63.

Panksepp, J. (2006) 'Emotional endophenotypes in evolutionary psychiatry.' *Progress in Neuro-Psychopharmacolgy & Biological Psychiatry*, 30: pp.774–84.

Panksepp, J. (2010) 'Affective neuroscience of the emotional BrainMind: evolutionary perspectives and implications for understanding depression.' *Dialogues in Clinical Neuroscience*, 12.4: pp.533–45.

pp.108-109 Human vs dog emotions

Andics, A., Gácsi, M., Faragó, T., Kis, A. & Miklósi, A. (2014) 'Voice-Sensitive Regions in the Dog and Human Brain Are Revealed by Comparative fMRI.' *Current Biology*, 24.5: pp.574-78.

Berns, G., Brooks, A. & Spivak, M. (2015) 'Scent of the familiar: An fMRI study of canine brain responses to familiar and unfamiliar human and dog odors.' *Behavioural Processes*, 110: pp.37–46.

Horowitz, A. (2007) 'Anthropomorphism' in Bekoff, M. (ed.) *Encyclopedia of Human-Animal Relationships.* Westport, CT: Greenwood Publishing Group.

Horowitz, A.C. and Bekoff, M. (2007) 'Naturalizing anthropo-morphism: behavioral prompts to our humanizing of animals.' *Anthrozoös*, 20.1: pp.23-35.

Midgley, M. (2002) *Beast and Man.* London: Routledge.

Serpell, J. A. (2002). 'Anthropomorphism and anthropomorphic selection beyond the "cute response".' *Society & Animals*, 11.1: pp.83-100.

pp.110-111 Emotional body language

Quaranta, A., Siniscalchi, M. & Vallortigara, G. (2007) 'Asymmetric tail-wagging responses by dogs to different emotive stimuli.' *Current Biology*, 17.6: pp.R199-R201.

pp.112-113 How do you feel?

Harris, C.R., Prouvost, C. (2014) 'Jealousy in Dogs.' *PLoS ONE* 9(7): e94597. DOI:10.1371.

Mendl, M., Brooks, J., Basse, C., *et al.* (2010) 'Dogs showing separation-related behaviour exhibit a "pessimistic" cognitive bias.' *Current Biology*, 20.19: pp.39-40.

Range, F., Horn, L., Viranyi, Z., & Huber, L. (2008) 'The absence of reward induces inequity aversion in dogs.' *Proceedings of the National Academy of Sciences (PNAS)*, 106.1: pp.340-45.

Seligman, M.E, Maier, S.F. & Geer, J.H. (1968) 'Alleviation of learned helplessness in the dog.' *Journal of Abnormal Psychology*, 73.3, Part 1: pp.256-62.

pp.114-115 Analysing behaviour

Friedman, S.G. (2007) 'A Framework for Solving Behavior Problems: Functional Assessment and Intervention Planning.' *Journal of Exotic Pet Medicine*, 16.1: pp.6-10.

Friedman, S. G. (2009) 'Behavior fundamentals: Filling the behavior-change toolbox.' *Journal of Applied Companion Animal Behavior*, 3.1: pp.36-40.

pp.116-117 Gender differences

Dunbar, I. (1999) *Dog Behaviour*. New York: Howell Book House.

Heidenberger, E., and Unshelm, J. (1990) 'Changes of behaviour in dogs after castration.' *Tierarztliche Praxis*, 13.1: pp.69-75.

O'Heare, J. (2006) 'The Effects of Spaying and Neutering on Canine Behavior' in O'Heare, J. *Aggressive Behavior in Dogs* (2nd edition, 2014). Kindle edition.

Sanborn, L.J. (2007) *'Long-term health risks and benefits associated with spay/neuter in dogs.'* Published online: http://www.naiaonline.org/pdfs/althEffectsOfSpayNeuterInDogs.pdf (accessed 22.2.16).

pp.118-119 What can you change?

Ostrander, E.A., Giger, U. & Lindblad-Toh, K. (eds) (2006) *The Dog and its Genome*. New York: Cold Spring Harbor Laboratory Press.

Parker, H., Sutter, N. & Ostrander, E. (2005) 'Understanding Genetic Relationships among Purebred Dogs' in Ostrander, E.A., Giger, U. & Lindblad-Toh, K. (eds) *The Dog and its Genome*. New York: Cold Spring Harbor Laboratory Press.

Våge, J., Bønsdorff, T.B., Arnet, E., Tverdal, A. & Lingaas, F. (2010) 'Differential gene expression in brain tissues of aggressive and non-aggressive dogs.' *BMC Veterinary Research*, 6.34.

Willis, M.B. (1995) 'Genetic aspects of dog behaviour with particular reference to working ability' in Serpell, J.A. (ed.) *The Domestic Dog: its Evolution, Behaviour, and Interactions with People*. Cambridge: Cambridge University Press.

pp.120-21 Keeping yourself fit

Cutt, H., Giles-Corti, B., & Knuiman, M. (2008) 'Encouraging physical activity through dog walking: Why don't some owners walk with their dog?' *Preventive Medicine*, 46.2: pp.120-26.

The Gallup Organization. (2007) *Lifestyle Poll*. Washington DC: Gallup.

The People's Dispensary for Sick Animals (PDSA) *Animal Wellbeing (PAW) Report 2015*. Shropshire: PDSA.

Westgarth, C., Christley, R., & Christian, H. (2014) 'How might we increase physical activity through dog walking?' *International Journal of Behavioral Nutrition and Physical Activity*, 11:83. DOI: 10.1186.

pp.122-23 Keeping yourself busy

Bowman, A., *et al.* (2015) 'Four Seasons in an animal rescue centre; classical music reduces environmental stress in kennelled dogs.' *Physiology & Behavior*, 143: pp.70-82.

Schipper, L.L., *et al.* (2008) 'The effect of feeding enrichment toys on the behaviour of kennelled dogs (*Canis familiaris*).' *Applied Animal Behaviour Science*, 114.1: pp.182-95.

Wells, D. L., *et al.* (2002) 'The Influence of Auditory Stimualtion on the Behaviour of Dogs Housed in a Rescue Shelter.' *Animal Welfare*, 11: pp.385-93

Wagner, S., *et al.* (2004) *'BioAcoustic Research & Development (BARD) Canine Research Summary.'* Published online at http://throughadogsear.com/pdfs/BardExecutiveSummary.pdf (accessed 26.2.16).

pp.124-25 Going to school

Bennett, P., and Rohlf, V. (2007) 'Owner-companion dog interactions: Relationships between demographic variables, potentially problematic behaviours, training engagement and shared activities.' *Applied Animal Behaviour Science*, 102.1-2: pp.65-84.

Coren, S. (1999) 'Psychology applied to animal training' in Stec, A.M., Bernstein, D.A. (eds) *Psychology: Fields of Application*. Boston: Houghton Mifflin.

Hiby, E.F., Rooney, N.J. and Bradshaw, J.W.S. (2004) 'Dog training methods: their use, effectiveness and interaction with behaviour and welfare.' *Animal Welfare*, 13: pp.63-69.

Kass, P.H., New, J.C., Jr., Scarlett, J.M., & Salman, M.D. (2001) 'Understanding Animal Companion Surplus in the United States: Relinquishment of Nonadoptables to Animal Shelters for Euthanasia.' *Journal of Applied Animal Welfare Science*, 4.4: pp.237-48.

The People's Dispensary for Sick Animals (PDSA) *Animal Wellbeing (PAW) Report 2015*. Shropshire: PDSA.

pp.132-33 What motivates you?

Bradshaw, J., Blackwell, E. and Casey, R. (2009) 'Dominance in domestic dogs – useful construct or bad habit?' *Journal of Veterinary Behavior*, 4.3: pp.135-44.

James Serpell (ed.) (1995) *The Domestic Dog: Its Evolution, Behaviour and Interactions with People*. Cambridge: Cambridge University Press.

Landsberg, G., Hunthausen, W. & Ackerman, L. (2003) *Handbook of Behavior Problems in the Dog and Cat*. Philadelphia, PA: W.B. Saunders.

Parker, G.A. (1974) Assessment strategy and the evolution of animal conflicts. *Journal of Theoretical Biology*, 47: pp.223-43.

pp.136-37 Dogs as teachers

Duranton, C. and Gaunet, F. (2015) *'Canis sensitivus*: Affiliation and dogs' sensitivity to others' behavior as the basis for synchronization with humans?' *Journal of Veterinary Behavior: Clinical Applications and Research*, 10.6: pp.513-24.

Fugazza, C. and Miklósi, A. (2014) 'Should old dog trainers learn new tricks? The efficiency of the Do as I do method and shaping/clicker training method to train dogs.' *Applied Animal Behaviour Science*, 153: pp.53-61.

pp.138-39 Playtime with other dogs

Bekoff, M. (2004) 'Wild justice and fair play: cooperation, forgiveness, and morality in animals.' *Biology & Philosophy*, 19: pp.489-520.

Fagen, R. (1981) *Animal Play Behavior*. New York: Oxford University Press.

Horowitz, A.C. (2002) *'The behaviors of theories of mind, and*

a case study of dogs at play.' Ph.D. thesis, University of California, San Diego.

Garvey, C. (1976) 'Some properties of social play' in Bruner, J., Jolly, A. and Sylva, K. (eds) *Play – Its Role in Development and Evolution*. New York: Basic Books Inc.

Tomasello, M., Call, J., Nagell, K., Olguin, R. and Carpenter, M. (1994) 'The learning and use of gestural signals by young chimpanzees: A trans-generational study.' *Primates*, 35: pp.137-54.

Ward, C., Bauer, E.B. & Smuts, B.B. (2008) 'Partner preferences and asymmetries in social play among domestic dog, *Canis lupus familiaris*, littermates.' *Animal Behaviour*, 76.4: pp.1187-99.

pp.144-45 Your human family

Guo, K., Meints, K., Hall, C., Hall, S. & Mills, D. (2009) 'Left gaze bias in humans, rhesus monkeys and domestic dogs.' *Animal Cognition*, 12: pp.409-18.

Téglás, E., *et al.* (2012) 'Dogs' gaze following is tuned to human communicative signals.' *Current Biology*, 22.3: pp.209-12.

pp.146-47 What family do you need?

Workman, L. and Fearon, J. (2012) Study conducted in collaboration with the Kennel Club and OnePoll and presented to the British Psychological Society Annual Conference in London, 20 April 2012.

pp.148-49 Working for humans

Guide Dogs for the Blind Association (2014). *Guide Dogs Annual Report and Accounts 2014*. Reading: Guide Dogs for the Blind Association.

pp.150-51 Relaxing and sharing

Hare, B., and Tomasello, M. (1999) 'Domestic dogs (*Canis familiaris*) use human and conspecific social cues to locate hidden food.' *Journal of Comparative Psychology*, 113.2: p.173.

Kikusui, T., Nagasawa, M., Onaka, T. and Ohta, M. (2009) 'Dog's gaze at its owner increases owner's urinary oxytocin during social interaction.' *Hormones and Behavior*, 55:3, pp.434-41.

Nagasawa, M. et al. (2015) 'Oxytocin-Gaze Positive Loop and the Coevolution of Human-Dog Bonds.' *Science*, 348.6232: pp.333-36.

Oliva, J. L., *et al.* (2015) 'Oxytocin enhances the appropriate use of human social cues by the domestic dog (*Canis familiaris*) in an object choice task.' *Animal cognition,* 18.3: pp.767–75.

The People's Dispensary for Sick Animals (PDSA) *Animal Wellbeing (PAW) Report 2015.* Shropshire: PDSA.

pp.152-53 Influencing humans

American Academy of Pediatrics. (2015) 'Research suggests canine companionship helps calm children undergoing cancer treatment.' *ScienceDaily,* 23 October 2015. Published online at https://www.sciencedaily.com/eleases/2015/10/151023083252.htm (accessed 22.2.16).

Nightingale, F. (1859) *Notes on Nursing.* London: Harrison.

McCullough, A. (2015) '*The Effects of Animal-Assisted Interventions (AAIs) for Pediatric Oncology Patients, Their Parents, and Therapy Dogs at Five Hospital Sites.'* Paper presented at the American Academy of Pediatrics (AAP) National Conference & Exhibition in Washington, DC on 25 October 2015.

Serpell, J. A. (1991) 'Beneficial effects of pet ownership on some aspects of human health and behaviour.' *Journal of the Royal Society of Medicine,* 84: pp.717–20.

Tonoike A. (2015) 'Comparison of owner-reported behavioral characteristics among genetically clustered breeds of dog (Canis familiaris).' *Scientific Reports, 5,* Article no.17710. DOI:10.1038.

Wells, D.L. (2007) 'Domestic dogs and human health.' *British Journal of Health Psychology,* 12: pp.145–56.

Wells, D.L. (2009) 'The effects of animals on human health and well-being.' *Journal of Social Issues,* 65: pp.523–43.

pp.154-55 Playing with humans

Horowitz, A.C. and Bekoff, M. (2007) 'Naturalizing anthropomorphism: behavioral prompts to our humanizing of animals.' *Anthrozoös,* 20.1: pp.23–35.

Mitchell, R.W. and Thompson, N.S. (1991) 'Projects, routines, and enticements in dog-human play' in Bateson, P.P.G. and Klopfer, P.H. (eds) *Perspectives in Ethology.* New York: Plenum Press.

Rooney, N., Bradshaw, J. and Robinson, I. (2000) 'A comparison of dog-dog and dog-human play behaviour.' *Applied Animal Behaviour Science,* 66: pp.235–48.

pp.158-59 Aches and pains

O'Neill, D.G. *et al.* (2013) 'Longevity and mortality of owned dogs in England.' *The Veterinary Journal,* 198.3: pp.638–643.

Michell, A.R. (1999) 'Longevity of British breeds of dog and its relationships with sex, size, cardiovascular variables and disease.' *Veterinary Record,* 145.22: pp.625–29.

Hall, J.A., et al. (2010) 'Aged Beagle dogs have decreased neutrophil phagocytosis and neutrophil-related gene expression compared to younger dogs.' *Veterinary immunology and immunopathology,* 137.1: pp.130–35.

Larsen, J.A. and Farcas, A. (2014) 'Nutrition of aging dogs.' *Veterinary Clinics of North America: Small Animal Practice,* 44.4: pp.741–59.

pp.160-61 Ageing brain and senses

Gelatt, K.N. (ed.) (2014). *Veterinary Ophthalmology (3rd edition).* Iowa: John Wiley and Sons Inc.

Salvin, H. et al. (2010) 'Under diagnosis of canine cognitive dysfunction: A cross-sectional survey of older companion dogs.' *The Veterinary Journal,* 184: pp.277–81.

pp.162-63 Keeping happy in old age

The Kennel Club (UK) (2015) *Do you know how to look after your dog in its senior years?* London: The Kennel Club.

pp.164-65 Time to say goodbye

Katcher, A.H., and Rosenburg, M.A. (1979) 'Euthanasia and the management of the client's grief.' *Compendium on Continuing Education,* 1: pp.887–91.

Planchon, L.A. *et al.* (2002) 'Death of a companion cat or dog and human bereavement.' *Psychosocial variables.' Society & Animals,* 10.1: pp.93–105.

Walker, J., Waran, N. and Phillips, C. (2014) 'The effect of conspecific removal on the behaviour and physiology of pair-housed shelter dogs.' *Applied Animal Behaviour Science,* 158: pp.46–56.

Wrobel, T. and Dye, A. (2003) 'Grieving Pet Death: Normative, Gender and Attachment Issues.' *OMEGA,* 47.4: pp.385–93.

Villalobos A. and Kaplan, L. (2007) *Canine and Feline Geriatric Oncology: Honoring the Human-Animal Bond.* Hoboken, NJ: Wiley-Blackwell, with permission.

pp.168-69 Travel troubles

AAA Foundation for Traffic Safety. (2011) *AAA/Kurgo online survey, 2011.*

American Pet Products Association (APPA). *2013-2014 APPA National Pet Owners Survey.* Connecticut: American Pet Products Association Inc.

Blunck, H., Owsley, C., MacLennan, P.A. & McGwin, G. (2013) 'Driving with Pets as a Risk Factor for Motor Vehicle Collisions among Older Drivers.' *Accident Analysis & Prevention,* 58: pp.70–74.

Petplan (2011). *Petplan Pet Census 2011.* Published online at: https://www.petplan.co.uk/petcensus/censusinfo.pdf (accessed 22/2/16).

The People's Dispensary for Sick Animals (PDSA) *Animal Wellbeing (PAW) Report 2015.* Shropshire: PDSA.

pp.170-71 Don't leave me

Appleby, D. and Pluijmakers, J. (2003) 'Separation anxiety in dogs.' *Veterinary Clinics of North America, Small Animal Practice,* 33.2: pp.321–44.

Borchelt, P.L. and Voith, V.L. (1982) 'Diagnosis and treatment of separation-related behavior problems in dogs.' *The Veterinary clinics of North America, Small Animal Practice,* 12.4: p.625.

Dogs Trust. *Beating Boredom.* Published online at: https://www.dogstrust.org.uk/help-advice/factsheets-downloads (accessed 22.2.16).

Horwitz, D.F. and Neilson, J.C. (eds). (2013) *Blackwell's Five-minute Veterinary Consult Clinical Companion: Canine and Feline Behavior.* New Jersey: John Wiley & Sons.

The People's Dispensary for Sick Animals (PDSA) *Animal Wellbeing (PAW) Report 2015.* Shropshire: PDSA.

Tuber, Davis S., et al. (1996) 'Behavioral and glucocorticoid responses of adult domestic dogs (*Canis familiaris*) to companionship and social separation.' *Journal of Comparative Psychology,* 110.1: p.103.

pp.172-73 Frustrated and bored

Satoshi, I. and Panksepp, J. (1992) 'The effects of early social isolation on the motivation for social play in juvenile rats.' *Developmental Psychobiology,* 25.4: pp.261–74.

pp.174-75 Aggressive behaviour

Bradshaw, J.W.S., McPherson, J.A., Casey, R.A., & Larter, I.S. (2002). 'Aetiology of separation-related behaviour in domestic dogs.' *Veterinary Record,* 151: pp.43–46.

Casey, R.A., Loftus, B., Bolster, C., Richards, G.J., & Blackwell, E.J. (2014) 'Human directed aggression in domestic dogs (*Canis familiaris*): Occurrence in different contexts and risk factors.' *Applied Animal Behaviour Science,* 152: pp.52–63.

Millsopp, S., Westgarth, C., Barclay, R. & Ward, M. (2012) *Association of Pet Behaviour Counsellors: Annual Review of Cases 2012.* Llanelli, UK: APBC.

pp.176-77 Afraid and anxious

Steimer T. (2002) 'The biology of fear- and anxiety-related behaviors.' *Dialogues in Clinical Neuroscience,* 4.3: pp.231–49.

pp.178-79 Dogs and children

American Veterinary Medical Association Task Force on Canine Aggression and Human-Canine Interaction. (2001) 'A Community Approach to Dog Bite Prevention.' *JAVMA,* 218.11: pp.1732–46.

pp.180-81 Other scary things

Brait, E. (2015) 'Canine PTSD: how the US military's use of dogs affects their mental wellbeing.' *The Guardian,* 11 November 2015.

Dreschel, N.A. (2010) 'The effects of fear and anxiety on health and lifespan in pet dogs.' *Applied Animal Behaviour Science,* 125.3: pp.157–62.

Overall, K. (2013) *Manual of Clinical Behavioral Medicine for Dogs and Cats.* Missouri: Elsevier, Mosby.

Index